CREATING **DESIGN**

THINKING LEARNING

JOURNEYS **FOR**

TRAINING THAT

GET **AND**

DEVELOPMENT RESULTS

SHARON BOLLER 🍷 LAURA FLETCHER

atd
PRESS
Alexandria, VA

ATD Press is an internationally renowned source of insightful and practical information on talent development, training, and professional development.

The content in chapter 13 is published with permission of the California Independent System Operator Corp. All rights reserved.

Chapter 14 was written by Sharon Boller, Beth Boller, and Kristen Hewett. Images within chapter 14 are used with permission from NxStage Medical, Inc.

Appendix 11 content developed by Will Thalheimer with help from others. Version 12. © Copyright 2018. Info: worklearning.com/ltem/

ATD Press
1640 King Street
Alexandria, VA 22314 USA

Ordering information: Books published by ATD Press can be purchased by visiting ATD's website at td.org/books or by calling 800.628.2783 or 703.683.8100.

Library of Congress Control Number: 2020934144

ISBN-10: 1-95049-618-X
ISBN-13: 978-1-950496-18-1
e-ISBN: 978-1-950496-19-8

ATD Press Editorial Staff
Director: Sarah Halgas
Manager: Melissa Jones
Community of Practice Manager, Learning Design: Eliza Blanchard
Developmental Editor: Jack Harlow
Production Editor: Hannah Sternberg
Text Design: Michelle Jose, Stephanie Shaw
Cover Design: Faceout Studio, Amanda Hudson
Printed by Versa Press, East Peoria, IL

Contents

Introduction

The stories captivated us. The first one was the story of Doug Dietz, an industrial designer for GE Health. He shared it in a TED Talk as he described his pride in his design of an MRI machine. His pride turned to distress as he stood in a hospital hallway and watched a young child crying as she approached the MRI scanning room with her parents (TEDx San Jose 2012).

As they neared the entrance to the MRI room, the dad bent down to his daughter and said, "Remember, we talked about how you need to be brave." The machine Doug so proudly designed terrified young patients (and even adult ones) when they needed a scan. Eighty percent of kids required sedation to successfully get a scan. Doug was mortified and vowed to redesign the experience of getting a scan by involving those who feared it the most: preschoolers. The result of this design-thinking approach to redesigning the experience of a scan meant that one hospital reduced its sedation rate from 80 percent to 1 percent.

The second story happened at Stanford University, where a class was challenged with designing a cheaper incubator. One team went to Nepal, where they visited the rural communities where babies were most at risk of dying from premature birth or low birth weight. In observing the communities and talking with these families, they realized the task wasn't just to build a cheaper incubator, it was to design one that was accessible to families who would never make it to a hospital. The biggest constraint was environment, not cost (ABC News 2011). Their human-centered, design-thinking approach gave them completely different insight into how to solve the problem. Instead of a high-tech, sleek incubator made with low-cost parts, they created a low-tech incubator that looked like a small sleeping bag and maintained an infant's body temperature for four hours. It could be recharged for another four hours by putting it into boiling water for a few minutes. The Embrace Nest infant warmer has helped more than 200,000 babies (Extreme Design for Extreme Affordability; Standford University).

In training and development, our stories may be less dramatic, but there is a desperate need for a human-centered approach to designing learning. Our industry tends to think first about creating courses and workshops instead of recognizing learning as a journey that involves many steps and stages. The experiences we have at each stage of the journey either propel us forward or cause us to exit. We spend billions of dollars each year on training solutions without significant success stories to share in terms of results or rave reviews from learners. That's a problem if people opt out of the journey or the journey leads to nowhere. When that happens, we have failed our learners and our organizational needs.

This book offers a primer on how to apply design thinking techniques to training and performance development. Design thinking is a problem-solving methodology that focuses heavily on involving users of a solution in its design. We start with a brief primer on design thinking and then introduce you to our LXD Framework, a way of integrating design thinking techniques with instructional design. We show and tell how to use a variety of tools that can help you create an optimal learning experience. For us, optimal learning experience means three things:

- It delivers value to learners.
- It solves a problem for the organization.
- It produces a measurable outcome.

And note how we frame it as a learning experience. We don't create learning. Instead, people have an experience as they learn. The learning typically comes from a variety of means, including formal training programs, resources, and experiences. At times you will see learning experience design referenced. Other times we may reference training. When we reference training, we are talking about a formal event. When we reference a learning experience, we are talking about a collection of activities that a learner participates in or has access to that support learning something.

Design thinking can be for anyone in training and performance development, which itself encompasses a lot of roles and titles. Are you a learning designer, learning architect, instructional designer, L&D professional, HR professional, chief learning officer, training professional, or talent development professional? Our industry uses lots of different acronyms and role titles. For clarity's sake, we reference training and performance development professionals to encompass all these possible roles. This book is for you.

Here's what you'll find within this book:

- **Section 1: Get Acquainted With the Concepts** summarizes what design thinking is and how to connect its steps to training and performance development. This section also introduces our learning experience design (LXD) framework as a means of incorporating design thinking techniques within the process of training program and learning experience design.

- **Section 2: Get Perspective and Refine the Problem** focuses on the early steps in the framework. It includes tools that help you gather perspective from all the stakeholders associated with a request for training and helps you refine the problem for which training was predefined as a solution.

- **Section 3: Ideate, Prototype, and Iterate** contains tools that help you involve your learner and business stakeholders in designing, developing, and testing your solution.

- **Section 4: Implement and Evaluate** walks you through what's needed to ensure people benefit from what you developed. Within it, we provide tools and techniques for activating what you've designed and measuring your impact.

- **Section 5: Sell Your Use Case** offers insights on how to sell the use of design thinking techniques to develop training solutions within your organization. It includes two case studies you can use to help showcase the power of design thinking in training and development.

Armed with the concepts and techniques in this book, you can move beyond creating events to creating experiences that produce measurable results.

SECTION 1

GET ACQUAINTED WITH THE CONCEPTS

① A Primer on Design Thinking

In This Chapter:
- How and why learning solutions fail
- An antidote to failure: design thinking and its "sweet spot"
- The five keys to design thinking

Imagine that you and your friend Suzy agree to go on a vacation together. Suzy is all-in on the idea of a friend vacation, but she's not much into planning. "No worries," you tell Suzy. "I love planning trips. I'll take care of everything. All you have to do is show up." Because you want to ensure you both have a great vacation, you agree on the timing, climate, and budget, but you tell Suzy to trust you for the rest.

You dive into planning. You find a perfect hiking trip for the two of you. Suzy and you have gone on a couple hikes before and seemed to have fun, so you are confident she'll love it. Your week-long trip features daily long hikes, tent camping, and backpacking your supplies between camping destinations. Your trip will be a fantastic respite from the frenzy of daily life. The campsites you'll stay at are primitive and have no electricity. There is no cell phone reception either, ensuring you get fully off the grid.

The designated day of departure arrives. You reached out to Suzy a few days prior and told her to meet you at the airport at 8 a.m. with shorts, t-shirts, and hiking shoes. There's no mention of any other type of clothing, which is when Suzy starts to get a bit nervous. However, she arrives at the appointed time and you excitedly share your destination and itinerary. Suzy's face says it all: She's horrified. She lets you know she H-A-T-E-S camping. Her idea of "active" differs dramatically from yours. To her, a couple of three-mile hikes in a week is active, particularly if coupled with a leisurely day of pedaling a bike around a cute little seaside resort town. She wants a hot shower and a

3

clean, cozy bed every night. Finally, she has no desire to carry her food—she wants it served in a restaurant.

What the heck happened? You thought you had good info on Suzy, but you made several assumptions fueled by limited facts. With those assumptions, you proceeded to plan a vacation that did not match her wants or needs. The result was an unsatisfactory vacation for both of you, as neither of you got what you wanted or needed from it.

Right now, you are probably thinking, "I would never do this. Obviously, someone who is going on a vacation needs to give input into the destination and the activities. Otherwise, it will be a horrible experience for that person. This is a crazy, unrealistic example."

You're right. It is crazy.

But guess what? People inside companies do different versions of this kind of crazy all the time.

How and Why Learning Fails to Be a Solution

If you're reading this book, you are likely looking for a way to make a training or performance development solution produce bonafide performance and operational results for your company. If you are like us, there are three possible ways to sabotage your efforts:

- **You fail to clarify exactly what results the company wants to attain.** You lack knowledge of the needs of the business: the "why" of the solution from the business's perspective and what operational result the business hopes to achieve. If no one can specify the destination, it's difficult to design a journey to get there.
- **You make assumptions about learners instead of gathering perspective from them.** You gather demographic data (experience, education, tenure) and you even craft learning objectives. What you miss doing is diving deep into empathy-building. You don't take time (or don't feel you have the time) to get perspective from learners on their daily realities: what they think, feel, see, hear, and do related to whatever you're focusing on helping them learn. You don't fully understand the context in which they will be

asked to apply what they learn or what constraints their real world may pose in doing that application. When you don't gather input into their attitudes and daily worldview, you must instead rely on assumptions: either yours or those of a business stakeholder. You (and they) may be right, but statistically the odds are high that you are wrong. Relying on assumptions is dangerous territory to be in. Assumptions made with limited data tend to be wrong. The Amazon Fire phone is a great example of this and is referenced in two different business articles on the danger of assumptions (Forbes 2016; Fortune 2016).

- **You—and your stakeholders—focus on training as an event rather than a set of experiences.** This focus tempts you into designing stuff that people in your organization cannot easily implement or maintain. Learning is not an event that happens once and is done. It is a journey—a learner travels with a defined starting point and ending point and requires multiple opportunities to retrieve and practice use of learning along the way (Karpick and Roedinger 2008; UCLA's Bjork Learning Laboratory Research 2012). Training is commonly viewed as a business-centered process (BCP). It is designed as such, which means it usually is event-focused: a workshop, a conference, an e-learning course, or even a series of e-learning courses. It focuses exclusively on the business's needs or wants and doesn't typically consider the people who are the target of the event or solution.

The antidote to learning efforts that fail over and over? Design thinking and its "sweet spot."

How Do You Stop the Crazy?

Design thinking, in contrast to business-centered processes, is a human-centered process (HCP). It starts with a focus on people rather than the business desire for profit. It originated in the late 1950s as a problem-solving technique that quickly morphed into a product development technique. Companies realized that to create products that people would buy, they needed to start with the target user rather than the company's goal of making money. Profit would come from a solid understanding of what people wanted and needed and what their pain points were. Product developers needed to find a "sweet spot" between what target buyers would find useful, what a company could profitably make, and how that product could be made within the constraints that both buyers and the business had. Its successful adoption in technology-based product development has pushed it to wider and wider usage across lots of sectors, including training and development. It's a natural fit because training and development already has processes that are similar. Design thinking provides a terrific overlay to existing training design processes and gives practitioners great tools and techniques to add to their toolbox.

The design thinking process provides a means for defining problems from multiple perspectives, brainstorming possible solutions, prototyping those solutions, and then testing and iterating to optimize the best approach. When you are creating training or job support tools, you can use tools and techniques from design thinking to design solutions that hit the "sweet spot" between three forces (Figure 1-1):

1. what the business wants or needs to achieve operationally (such as some sort of measurable goal)
2. what learners perceive as useful, relevant, engaging, and a valuable use of their time and effort
3. what can be realistically implemented and sustained given technology or environmental constraints that exist for the business and the targeted users.

For you to be effective at using design thinking steps and techniques, you need to understand each component of the Venn diagram, so let's dive a bit deeper.

Figure 1-1. Design Thinking Is About "Finding the Sweet Spot"

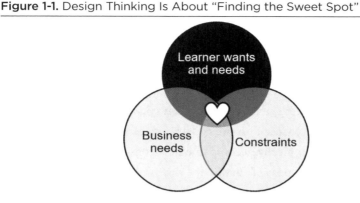

The Top Circle: Learner Wants and Needs

The simple definition of a great learning experience is one that:

- Delivers value to the learner (solves a problem they have). The learner may be an employee, a customer, a patient, or anyone who the business is trying to train to do something or help understand something.
- Is easy to use (avoids creating "miserable" moments due to clumsy or unclear directions).
- Is enjoyable to use (creates "magical moments" that delight the learner or make them want to continue their experience).

Think about Uber or Lyft and the app you use to request a ride from either company. First, that service—as represented by the app—solves a huge problem for many travelers: finding safe, reliable transportation when taxis aren't easily located. Second, the app is extremely easy to use; it is "intuitive," which means it doesn't require instructions. You learn how to use it by using it. Third, it's "enjoyable." You have the cool little map with the image of the car as it works its way toward you. You can see who your driver is, how others have rated that driver, and exactly what your trip will cost you. You don't have to tip or fumble with money. Those are all plusses that equate to "enjoyable."

Now think about a typical learning solution you might devise under the auspices of training and development. This solution might be an e-learning course or even an entire curriculum within your organization.

- What problem is the course or experience solving for the learner (not your organization)?
- What value is it providing to the learner?
- How enjoyable is it for the learner to complete?

Those are intriguing questions, because you likely don't consistently think of things from the learner's point of view when you design training. Instead, you are probably very focused on the constraints or the person making the request. Requests are typically accompanied by constraints. Therefore, you often think about what's possible within the timeline or budget you have. You think about what the business says the solution needs to include. You think about content that needs to go into it and how you'll get that content. You likely don't start with, "How would the learner describe this experience? Will they enjoy it? Find it valuable?"

Bottom-Line Performance (now merged with TiER1 Performance) does an annual learning trends survey. In 2018, it added a question specifically focused on the frequency with which learners were involved in a solution's design. The survey results suggest room for growth (Boller and Boller 2019). In many situations, subject matter experts (SMEs) and stakeholders claim the role of learner in the design meeting and assume they know what the learner wants, needs, and feels. No one verifies these assumptions with the learners themselves. Typically, this approach is well-intentioned: People want to save the learner's time. Unfortunately, making decisions based on assumptions about the learner's work context, constraints, wants, or needs leads to solutions that don't produce business results (and therefore don't meet the business needs). They also seldom meet learner needs and wants.

Take a look at the survey responses (Table 1-1). You'll see some positive trends here—and lots of room for growth. Given our own experience in the industry and the hundreds of projects we've been involved with, we know that it can be extremely challenging to get "voice of the learner" insights and perspectives. As we evaluated these results, we felt the *always* percentage was inflated.

Table 1-1. Bottom-Line Performance Annual Learning Trends Survey: Learning Involvement Question

2019: How often do you include target learners in your training design process?		
Answer Choices	Percent of Responses	Number of Responses
Always; target learner involvement is mandatory part of our process	26.17%	67
Usually; we try to do so every time, but sometimes it doesn't happen	32.81%	84
Sometimes; it depends on the initiative	28.52%	73
Occasionally; we only do so for very important initiatives	8.59%	22
Never	3.91%	10
Total respondents		256
2018: How often do you include target learners in your training design process?		
Answer Choices	Percent of Responses	Number of Responses
Very often	15.97%	19
Often	42.86%	51
Sometimes	20.17%	24
Rarely	18.49%	22
Never	2.52%	3
Total respondents		119

The Left Circle: Business Needs

Healthy businesses define financial targets they want to hit each year. They also usually have longer-term financial targets that are three to five years out. **The top-line financial target that businesses typically focus on is revenue and ways to increase it. The bottom-line financial target is profit and ways to increase profit margins and overall profits.** A focus on these two metrics helps ensure a company has enough cash and a good cash flow. Cash and cash flow (having enough cash to pay bills when bills are due) are the life blood of a business. Consequently, a lot of what a business does in terms of strategies and initiatives is with an eye toward growing revenue as well as increasing profits so that the business has enough cash to continue to operate and grow. Initiatives targeted toward improving employee engagement link back to revenue and profitability. Happy employees tend to be loyal, productive employees. Productive employees generate revenue and profit for the business.

Businesses typically have annual financial goals (cash, profit margin) they want to achieve. They then define business initiatives that support these financial—or operational—goals. Here are a couple of examples:

- A company's one-year financial goal might be to increase revenue by 20 percent (or perhaps to increase revenue related to a specific product by 20 percent). In support of that goal, the company might identify an initiative designed to help it either attract new customers or sell more goods or services to existing customers, such as launching a new product or service.
- A company's goal might be to increase its profit margin by 5 percent. While this can be attained by growing revenue, it might also be achieved by reducing the cost of delivering goods or services. One mechanism for reducing cost of goods or services is to adjust processes so those goods can be delivered more efficiently. Another mechanism for decreasing costs might be reducing ramp-up time for new hires so they reach maximum productivity more quickly. A third initiative might be to reduce quality problems, which also enables improved efficiency.

In short, business needs are typically driven by a need to increase revenue, improve cash flow, or improve profitability. Any training or learning solution you design should drive some sort of operational result, such as:

- increasing sales (which improves revenue, and, eventually, cash available to the business)
- speeding up the time it takes to close a sale or deliver a product (which improves cash flow)
- making someone or something (such as a process) more efficient (which lowers costs and improves profitability)
- increasing employee engagement, which can have a positive impact on employee retention as well as productivity.

C-suite leaders and upper-level managers must focus on business needs and results. This is not because they are solely focused on money. It's because they know jobs depend on this focus. If a company lacks enough cash or profitability, jobs are lost.

The Right Circle: Business and Learner Constraints

Decisions about how you will design, build, and deploy a solution must factor in constraints: learner, technical, environmental, and business.

These are common categories where constraints exist:

- **Time.** This includes time to create something, time required to implement something, time required to sustain something, time available to undergo a learning journey, and time available to support someone who is on a learning journey. It may also be a date by which something has to be done.
- **Budget.** What dollars are available to pay for development and implementation of a solution as well as ongoing maintenance of a solution? What return on investment does the company expect and how soon does it need to be achieved?
- **Skills.** What skills does the company have—or can gain access to—to design and build the solution?
- **Technology.** What software, hardware, and device limitations exist?
- **Access to needed people or other resources.** People you need access to include stakeholders who pave the way for a project to get done, subject matter experts who contribute insights, and target learners who provide perspective. Other resources you may need access to include space and testing tools.

There's a cautionary tale in discussing constraints. Often people assume there are constraints that may not really exist. Constraints should always be verified by those who are assumed to be creating them. Go ahead and brainstorm all the constraints you can think of; just check them all out before assuming they are all correct.

The Five Steps to Design Thinking

We've outlined the problem we hope to solve with this book: shifting from a sole focus on the business or content when designing learning experiences to a learner-focused approach that gets to a win-win for learners and the business. We've also explained the three factors practitioners need to balance to remedy this problem.

The question remains: How exactly does one go about "finding the sweet spot?"

The rest of the book provides answers as well as examples. Before we move on, though, we want to give you a quick primer on the traditional design thinking model that served as our starter for modifying how we design a better learner experience. The model features five steps: empathize, define, ideate, prototype, and test (Figure 1-2).

Figure 1-2. Traditional Illustration of Design Thinking Approach to Product Development

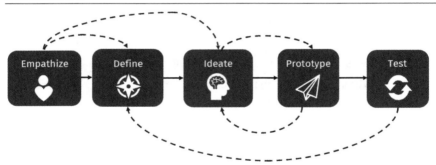

Design thinking does not have its origins in design; it's a problem-solving approach that's been around for decades and has uses across lots of industries. It's most useful when problems or optimal solutions are fuzzy. It's human-centered, which means it starts by focusing on people rather than business goals. Product developers often use a design thinking approach to design products because the products ideally solve some sort of problem or need that buyers or users have.

Product developers take an iterative journey through these steps:

- In the **empathize** step, designers spend time gaining perspective from target users of a potential need that a product might solve. This perspective-gathering process, done via observations or interviews, enables them to build empathy for the users and their wants and needs. During this step, designers spend time observing users in their environment so they can see potential needs or problems in the context of the user's daily experience. They interview them, asking questions about their likes and dislikes, their thoughts and feelings, their pain points, and their motivators. They build a clear picture of how people might use a potential product and what value the product can provide—from the user's perspective.

- The second step is to **define** a problem that exists from both the business's perspective and the user's perspective. Here's where business goals enter the picture. A user may have a need, but the business must be able to solve that need while also making a profit. Once this problem (or opportunity) is defined and constraints begin to emerge (for example, the product must be portable; it cannot cost more than $X to produce, and so on), designers can begin to . . .

- **Ideate** and brainstorm possible solutions to the problem, seeking solutions and ideas that fit within that sweet spot of user needs, business needs, and technology or environmental constraints.

- The next step is to **prototype**—quickly and cheaply—the most promising and intriguing solutions.

- Target users then **test** these solutions. Designers seek user feedback and observe users interacting with the prototypes, weighing user feedback against technical constraints and business needs.

- Observation and user feedback help designers **iterate** on their original ideas and prototypes, making improvements that align with the sweet spot they are trying to stay within. Implementation is implied but not really stated. That's because some products continuously iterate (think software-as-a-service products that push out new releases every few weeks to months).

Work on Your Own

Think about a product or service that you love, whether it's Uber, the Starbucks app, an online grocery ordering service, a life-changing childcare product, or even a great restaurant that you frequent.

Consider why you love it. What need or want is it satisfying for you? What need does the service satisfy for the business? And what constraints are factored into that product or service's design?

Your needs drive your use of the product or service—not the needs of the business. In the same way, the learners' needs will drive the value they receive from whatever solutions you create, not the needs of the business.

Summary

In this chapter we introduced you to the fallacy of trying to design solutions without considering the needs of the end user. Just like you shouldn't plan a vacation without consulting the other vacationers, organizations need to avoid designing training programs and learning solutions without input from learners.

We then walked you through a problem-solving approach that brings users of a solution into the process of designing that solution: design thinking. Its starting point of "empathize" helps designers create a balance between users, the business, and environmental constraints. In chapter 2, we'll talk about how to take this basic design thinking model and use it to develop more learner-centered solutions, shifting away from a primarily business-focused model to one that equally balances the needs of learners with the needs of the business.

Linking Design Thinking to Learning Experiences

In This Chapter:
- Why design thinking matters for training and development
- The journey to actually learning something
- Magical versus miserable learning moments

We began adopting a design thinking approach to training design and performance development projects for two reasons:

- **Performance gaps are multi-faceted and traditional models
  don't recognize this complexity.** David Wile's model of human
  performance factors illustrates the complexity of performance very
  well. His updated model, published in 2014, identifies nine factors
  that influence performance with skills and knowledge only being
  one of those nine factors (Wile 2014). Too often, stakeholders either
  assume lack of skill is the cause of a problem or just turn to training
  as a "quick fix." Design thinking approaches engage the performers
  themselves to help uncover all the obstacles to performance, which
  likely involve some of Wile's other factors beyond skills and knowledge. When you avoid starting with the assumption that training is
  your best solution to a performance problem, you can better clarify
  what experiences will solve it. You can also ideate to see ways to
  combine initiatives that together form an optimal solution. See Figure 2-1 for the list of all nine factors and how Wile correlates them
  to ultimate organizational outputs and results.

- **Learning is experienced as a journey but organizations tend to think in terms of creating courses or events.** Design thinking approaches help counter "event" thinking. Design thinking doesn't assume the problem is obvious and only one possible solution exists. It helps stakeholders and targeted users (which for us equals learners) gain insight into each other and the problem to be solved. And it enables co-creation and frequent testing to ensure the solution will really solve the problem.

Figure 2-1. The Wile Human Performance Model

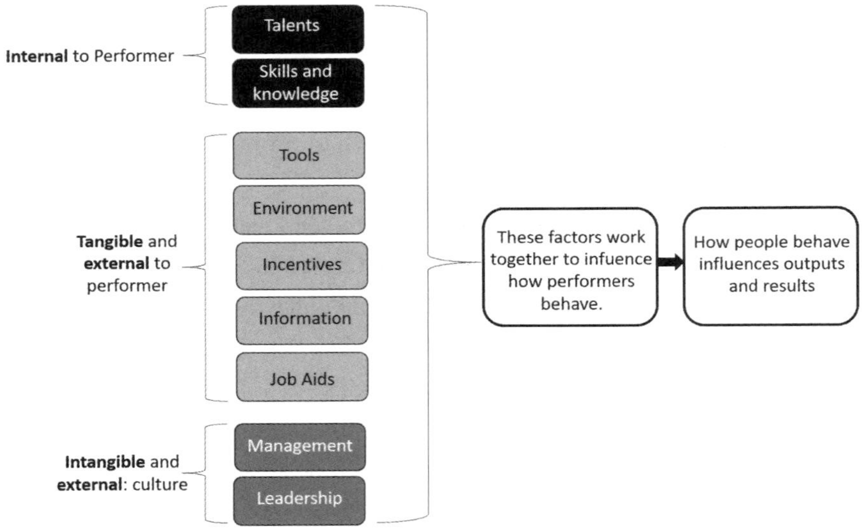

The Wile Human Performance Model helps us understand that our ability to perform our jobs depends on nine factors—not just one.

The Learning Journey

Let's consider that last bullet: learning is a journey, but it's treated like an event. Like you, we can get caught up in event-based planning. We, and often our customers, think of learning in terms of events that people do—an e-learning course, a workshop or a webinar, or perhaps a series of them—and then return to their job.

However, this approach runs counter to how people learn and remember for the long haul. People are hard-wired to forget things, not remember them. The brain has a lot of work to do in managing the influx of information it receives daily. Therefore, one key strategy it employs is to dismiss content or information that it never sees or hears about again (Medina 2014). Stuff that is part of an "event" often counts as this type of information if it isn't properly set up or reinforced through multiple opportunities to practice accessing it and using it (something known as retrieval practice). People's tendency to forget over time what they don't repeat is known as the forgetting curve.

To minimize or eliminate the forgetting curve, people need to recall information through multiple rounds of retrieval practice, a technique known as the spacing effect. People need stuff repeated multiple times to store it into their long-term memory and be able to retrieve it when they need it. The Get Real example "Forgetting Curve, Retrieval Practice, and Spacing Effect" dives into these concepts in further detail.

Get Real: Forgetting Curve, Retrieval Practice, and Spacing Effect

We throw some hefty learning science terms at you in this chapter. The best way to help you really understand these concepts is to take you all the way back to grade school. In grade school, most of you likely had a weekly spelling list. That list was introduced to you on Monday. You then had a test on your spelling words on Friday. If you only practiced spelling those words one time, you would likely fail your Friday spelling test. You most certainly would have forgotten the correct spellings of those words after a few weeks' time.

But most spelling lessons have you do a series of practice activities with the words designed to help you learn them—and remember them over time. For example, your teacher may have had you do what Sharon's teachers had her do:

- Review the words in class; discuss meaning (Monday lesson).
- Write each word five times (Monday night homework).
- Discuss the words and synonyms and antonyms for them (Tuesday lesson).
- Use each word in a sentence (Tuesday homework).

- Play a chalkboard relay game with the words (Wednesday lesson).
- Create flash cards and have someone quiz you on the words (Wednesday homework).
- Do a fill-in-the-blank activity using the words (Thursday lesson).
- Write a story using each word (Thursday homework).
- Take the test (Friday).

Your odds of forgetting how to spell the words decreased each day as you got spaced repetitions of them. This decreases the forgetting curve significantly. Every activity the teacher assigned provided retrieval practice. If you did the practice activities all week, you likely aced the end-of-week test.

Of course, if you never returned to those words—or used them in school or work later—you eventually might still forget them. However, with sufficient retrieval practice, knowledge and skills can be embedded into your memory for long periods of times, years after you first learned them. (To use another example, think about bike riding. You learn it as a child. If you did a lot of it growing up, you likely can get back on a bike and pick it up relatively quickly even if you let 20 years elapse before you try it again in adulthood.)

Here's a quote from a research summary collated by (some also performed by) UCLA's Bjork Learning and Forgetting Lab, which is named after cognitive psychologist Dr. Robert Bjork:

> The spacing effect is the finding that information that is presented repeatedly over spaced intervals is learned much better than information that is repeated without intervals (i.e., massed presentation). **This effect is one of the most robust results in all of cognitive psychology** and has been shown to be effective over a large range of stimuli and retention intervals from nonsense syllables (Ebbinghaus 1885) to foreign language learning across many months. (Bahrick, Bahrick, Bahrick, and Bahrick 1993; emphasis added)

In other words, learning is a journey, not an event.

This concept is critical to understand if you truly intend to affect business outcomes through training initiatives and learning experiences. Courses and workshops alone will not move the needle on performance change. Design thinking—with its emphasis on human-centered design and designing experiences—is a logical match when you recognize learners are on a journey and not just participating in events.

Figure 2-2 illustrates the learning journey we describe to clients to get them thinking about how to be intentional about the solution they craft. The metaphor of a map and a journey resonates, particularly when we explain that the stages of the journey correlate with the research on what's required for people to go from learning something to using it in their jobs consistently and well. You'll notice that it's not a straight line. People can—and often do—exit from the journey early, particularly if they are not fully engaged in it, don't find the content relevant to their needs, or realize that the use of of new skills or knowledge isn't supported by the organization.

Figure 2-2. The Four Stages in the Learning Journey

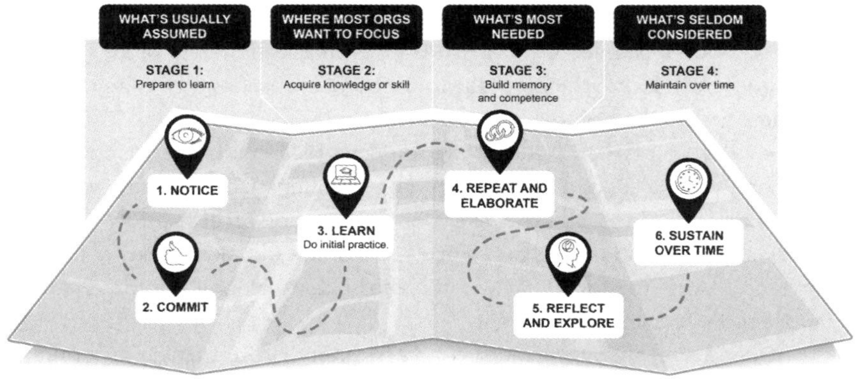

Getting a learner to stick with a journey to the end requires careful thought and planning as well as clarity on what will make the journey a relevant one for the learner.

Check out the Get Real sidebar "When There Is No Journey, Just an Event" for our own cautionary tale for treating training as a one-off event. With that lesson in mind, let's review each of the stages in the learning journey.

Get Real: When There Is No Journey, Just an Event

Within our organizations, we can struggle to plot out the entire learning journey and plan for the needed repetition and practice as well as long-term maintenance. We've both been part of initiatives with suboptimal rollouts as a result. Those failures can serve as a cautionary tale. Here's a particularly painful one.

Several years ago, as Bottom-Line Performance started growing beyond a handful of team members, we recognized the challenges people had in having "honest conversations" with one another when frustrations emerged during projects. People struggled to manage conflicts and interpersonal differences. Worse, when performance was a persistent problem, people weren't getting the feedback they needed to improve.

To address this, we rolled out a training program called Honest Conversations, and we created a mnemonic called SHARE to help people remember the steps to an honest conversation. We did role plays and practice within the session and we even printed job aids. We put every single company employee through it. After training, though, we had zero reinforcement. No spaced repetition. No proactive conversations within teams about successes using SHARE or even challenges in using it. No references to it when employees would bring a challenge to a manager. No help for employees to practice using it.

At the employees' request we did create a guidelines document to help people understand when conversations should stay within two teammates and when a situation might require escalation. These guidelines were added to our employee handbook, along with a copy of the SHARE model. That was the real extent of any reinforcement subsequent to the training event.

During a recent conversation five years after SHARE training occurred, we learned that our own senior leaders had forgotten about the model and couldn't recollect what was in the guidelines we created so long ago. They couldn't even remember what the mnemonic stood for. This is a painful example of our own failure. We created an event five years ago instead of designing a learning journey that could lead to sustained performance over time. Fast forward to today and we acknowledge we never solved the problem for which we designed an event years ago. That made our original investment a complete waste of everyone's time and our money.

Today, the SHARE model is dead, and people are still lacking skill in how to have the "honest conversations" that can make Bottom-Line Performance even more effective.

Stage 1: Prepare

The learning journey associated with formal events doesn't start when a learner starts the course but when the learner is getting ready to learn before the actual event. Designing for this stage requires that you get into the mind and heart of the learner. There are two steps within the stage:

- **Notice a need or opportunity to learn.** Learners may identify a need to learn from their own internal drive to build skill or knowledge. More frequently it is prompted by something happening within the organization, such as an initiative rolling out. Ideally, the goal is to stimulate motivation in learners rather than simply impose things onto them. "Everyone must complete this course by X date" is not motivating. Saying, "You are busy. This course can help make your daily job easier," might be more motivating. The notice stage is where learners' attention first gets grabbed. As the practitioner, you try to generate motivation or tap into motivation that may already exist. Optimally you appeal to a desire or need to master something. Learners who have a mastery goal and orientation (such as "I want to get good at this") achieve better long-term retention of whatever is taught than those with a compliance or performance orientation (such as "I need to meet a minimal standard, pass test, and so on" Murayama 2018).

- **Commit to learning whatever needs to be learned.** At this step the desired outcome is for a learner to commit to learning whatever it is that the organization needs for them to learn. Examples of commitment include signing up for a class, clearing a calendar to make time to study or to take a class, purchasing a book or course, and agreeing to be mentored. Continuing the theme of motivation, learners must have some level of motivation to move forward to committing. What's driving that motivation will affect attitude and openness to learning.

Training and development professionals make numerous assumptions at this stage. The most frequent is that they don't need to do much. A better strategy is to think like marketers and consider how you can draw attention to and cultivate interest in the benefits of learning something new. A marketing campaign for your training initiative can be a good way to cultivate positive feelings and avoid negative ones during this stage. At a minimum, a good marketing campaign can help learners understand why the content matters.

Stage 2: Acquire Knowledge or Skill

Acquiring knowledge or skill is usually the most structured portion of the learning journey. It involves conscious focus and attention to building new skills or absorbing new knowledge. It has a single step:

- **Learn and practice.** At this step, learners engage with the learning activities and materials and mentally involve themselves. It goes beyond attending physically to attending mentally and involves learners working to form connections with what they already know. We emphasize the phrase "mentally involved" because that is what people currently like to describe as "being engaged" in the material. What's really going on when people are engaged in training is that they are focusing mental attention on learning and fully participating in activities.

In the Get Real story about our failed learning event earlier in this chapter, we actually did a great job of designing this stage of the journey. We explained the SHARE model, let people discuss it and explain it in their words, and then gave them opportunities to practice doing it. People were highly involved and fully engaged throughout the training process. This mirrors what the graphic notes: People tend to put the most focus and time into designing the event.

The right things T&D practitioners do at this stage are to provide initial practice, along with opportunities to see worked examples of whatever is being taught. The wrong thing people sometimes do at this stage is being too focused on telling and thus spending little to no time letting people see demonstrations and practice themselves.

Stage 3: Build Memory and Try Using on the Job

This memory-building stage is where newly learned skills or knowledge become embedded into long-term memory. It is also where learners acquire the ability to retrieve the skills or knowledge when they get contextual cues to do so. Finally, it is where you can assess how well transfer to the workplace is happening. If you leave out stage 3 in the learning journey, you'll end up with results like those in our Get Real story about the failed training event: none.

The two steps within this stage will likely be interwoven. Repetition and elaboration help build memory. Reflection and exploration help deepen and broaden understanding as well as fully synthesize new learning with past or current practices. For example, the first few times you make a recipe, you may follow the steps exactly. Then after you repeat it a few times, you may attempt some elaborations, trying substitutions or shortcuts. As you do so, you may explore alternate versions of the recipe entirely or share your successes or setbacks with other cooks, helping them avoid your mistakes or repeat your successes. You may also connect two similar recipes, figuring out a better way to meet your specific goals.

- **Repeat and elaborate.** This step should be an opportunity for people to have additional safe practice. Learners may use a video rehearsal tool or have opportunities to do some recall practice on knowledge. The key is that this retrieval practice happens after a spaced interval in time. It's not right after the workshop or e-learning course; it's days to a couple of weeks afterward. You actually want some forgetting to happen. You want people to have to push themselves to remember and be reminded of the skill or appropriate knowledge as part of the practice. You also want there to be more than one repetition or opportunity. One pragmatic example comes from childhood math, where you learned multiplication tables over many repetitions spaced over time. Most of us can retrieve our knowledge of what 2 times 12 equals without much thought if we must figure out the cost of buying twelve $2 items in a store—$24.00. However, we didn't start out calculating multiples of things we were buying. We started out with multiplication problems on tests, chalkboard races in the classroom, and homework assignments.

- **Reflect and explore.** Once people have embedded knowledge or skills into their memory, you want to get them to extend the knowledge or skill. With this step, you want people to reflect on how well they are doing as they apply the skill in their jobs. For example, managers can observe and coach, providing feedback and asking employees to reflect on what they did well or how they executed each step of something. Practice without reflection and feedback is dangerous. What happens if someone practices something incorrectly? Reflection and exploration mean people get increasingly complex opportunities to practice and to reflect on their successes as well as things they need to improve doing. They also get to take something out of the safe space of training and implement it in real-world use cases. That real-world usage is what reinforces their ability to retrieve a skill or piece of knowledge when needed. This step can take a performer from "conscious competence" to "unconscious competence" over time. Unconscious competence means a person can proficiently perform a skill or retrieve knowledge without having to consciously think about it. (Recall when you no longer had to add numbers up on your fingers and could instead simply recall the answer to 5 plus 5 or 5 times 5 or 50 times 50. Or when you no longer need to look at a recipe to make a complex dish.)

In our Get Real story about the failed training event, we should have included some reinforcement and additional practice opportunities as part of regular team meetings. Alternately we could have set up a chat bot that gave video practice examples for people to engage with. Most importantly, we could have requested that managers routinely discuss the SHARE model with team members and invited those team members to share successes and misses with its use. We needed something to get people recalling the model and practicing its application. People's ability to recall things based on a cue or need in their work environment is central to assessing the effectiveness of any training they've had. If they can't retrieve it, they didn't learn it effectively. That likely means they went through a learning event but never had enough spaced retrieval practice to truly learn it for the long term. Once-and-done events—without multiple reinforcements—don't result in long-term learning.

Training and development professionals—often under pressure from stakeholders—sometimes eliminate these stages entirely. Failure to understand the forgetting curve, the criticality of retrieval practice, and the spacing effect are often reasons this stage gets eliminated or never gets considered. The likely impact is a wasted investment of everyone's time in developing and completing the training.

Stage 4: Maintain Over Time

This final stage is about ensuring people have the right support and resources to consistently perform the skills or use the knowledge they have acquired. It also is about ensuring that any "training for all" gets rolled out to each new hire that comes onboard after the initial group. This stage has a single step with a lot to it:

- **Support performance.** This gets into ensuring your ecosystem supports what you are asking people to do. That means people have appropriate infrastructure, resources, and performance supports. This has less to do with the learner and a lot to do with the organization that wants to see consistent performance. People do what is recognized, rewarded, and reinforced. They seldom do what is not. They also cannot do what they lack the resources to do. For example, if a product is unavailable to ship and has persistent shipping problems, a sales representative is unlikely to want to continue selling it. Instead they will rely on other products in the portfolio. Or, if an individual is told to always follow a safety standard and that safety standard adds time to a production schedule, then the production outputs need to be reduced to allow time for the safety procedure to be performed, or safety will slip. People do what they are rewarded for doing.

Think back to our Get Real story about the failed training event. We did nothing to maintain performance over time. Even if we had included several retrieval practices, we wouldn't have gotten to sustained performance over the long haul. Why? Because we didn't set up a good process or infrastructure to ensure ongoing usage of the SHARE model. We didn't require its usage; we didn't refer people back to it. We didn't coach to it on an ongoing basis when people presented challenges or conflicts. We didn't model it in meetings when conflicts arose. Finally, we didn't set up any metric to measure our success. We didn't describe what success was going to look like or how we would measure it.

Let's assume you do plan for all the stages and steps in the journey. Does that equal success?

Not quite: You also must think about maximizing the magical and avoiding the miserable.

Magical Versus Miserable

Magical and miserable is a concept borrowed from product design or customer experience mapping. Think about yourself as a consumer. You likely make purchase decisions based on how well-designed your buying journey is. For those who rely heavily on Amazon to make purchases, you are deciding that the experience of buying online is far more pleasant and convenient than the experience of driving to a store, parking the car, hunting for what you want, going to a checkout and paying for it, and then driving back home. Amazon has figured out ways to make what was miserable (time spent in the car and in traffic, time in a crowded store, difficulty in comparing items, and so on) into magical moments. Those magical moments likely propel you forward from browsing to buying.

Learning is no different. At various steps of the journey there are opportunities to create magical moments and circumvent miserable ones. Recognizing common miserable moments in a learning journey is a useful thing to ponder. Getting learners to tell you what's magical and what's miserable can help you create journeys that people are more likely to fully complete.

Work on Your Own

Use the learning journey worksheet in appendix 1 to think through a recent learning journey you've designed or been part of. Take time to reflect on things that made a particular step "magical" for you and things that might have made it a "miserable" one.

Table 2-1 lists magical and miserable moments we frequently hear people share when we ask them to do this task. See how many apply to the journey you map out.

Table 2-1. Common Magical and Miserable Moments

	Magical	Miserable
Notice	• Within notice step, the message is designed as a clever or humorous one that piques interest. • Within notice step, the messaging clearly communicates the "why" of the learning experience and how it benefits you and the organization. It explains the impact it can have.	• Email message: "You have been assigned the following course in the ACME LMS system. Please complete it by X date."
Commit	• Within commit step: Manager acknowledges the time required to participate in the learning experience. You are allowed to budget time to participate so it is not just extra hours you spend at work.	• No consideration for your schedule is made.
Learn and Practice	• Within learn and practice step, there is lots of demonstration and guided practice and not just tell. You get feedback as you practice. The scenarios are highly relevant to your job context.	• Lots of telling and little doing. Your specific job context isn't factored into any explanations.
Repeat and Elaborate	• Within the repeat and elaborate steps, you do some video coaching practices and get feedback. That feedback helps you transition to job usage.	• There is no repetition or follow-up of any kind.

Table 2-1. Common Magical and Miserable Moments (cont.)

	Magical	Miserable
Reflect and Explore	• Within reflect and explore you receive additional materials to help deepen knowledge. Someone who matters observes you on the job and asks you to reflect on your own performance.	• There is no follow-up of any kind. • You only hear about what you're doing wrong.
Sustain	• Within sustain, the existing incentives, processes, or infrastructure are adjusted to encourage use of the new skill.	• No one mentions the training again. • You were told to do a new skill, but no one rewards you for doing it.

Summary

This chapter covered a lot of ground. Most important, we helped you recognize learning as a journey rather than an event—and the science behind that journey. We discussed how turning miserable moments in training initiatives and learning experiences into magical ones can help propel your efforts. Finally, we invited you to work on your own to consider magical and miserable moments you have seen (and perhaps even designed) related to training and performance development experiences.

You're now ready to move to chapter 3 and consider the framework for integrating design thinking into training and development.

A Design Thinking Framework for Training and Development

In This Chapter:
- The rework of the design thinking model for training and performance development (T&D): the LXD framework
- The four principles that matter
- The LXD framework in action
- A design meeting agenda

Chapters 1 and 2 outlined the value in incorporating design thinking methods into training and development design efforts. Now it's time to consider what that looks like.

In our work with design thinking, we realized we needed to tweak the standard design thinking model for use in the realm of training and performance development. The baseline design thinking framework we overviewed in chapter 1 works well for product development and large-scale problem solving. However, it doesn't accurately mirror most T&D practitioners' reality. That reality is that the entire design process often starts with a request and usually an assumption that the problem is already defined. While the bones of the design thinking framework are sound, T&D professionals need a hybrid framework that also combines traditional instructional design practices. So we created the Learning Experience Design framework, or LXD for short. The LXD framework accounts for the initial request for training and blows out the iterative process in greater detail (Figure 3-1). It also calls out implementation as the final stage, something missing in the traditional design thinking approach to solving problems.

Figure 3-1. The LXD Framework for Learning and Performance Development Initiatives

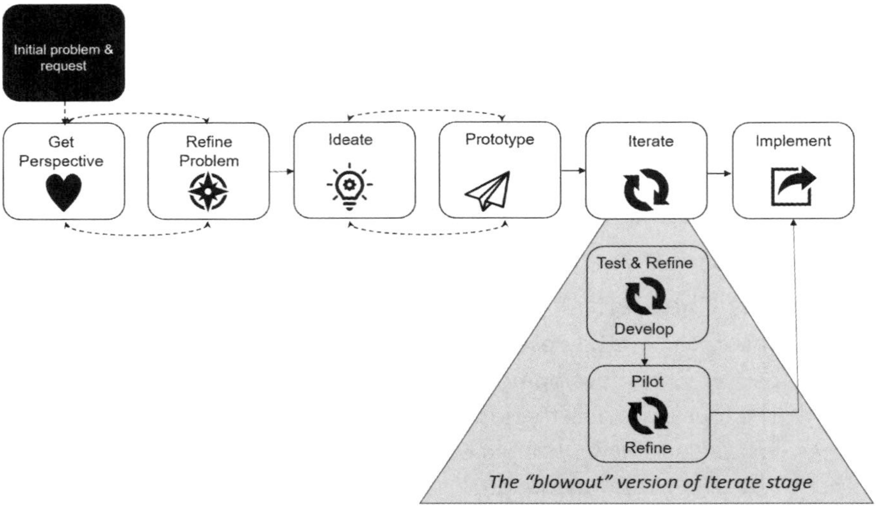

This framework combines a traditional ID approach and design thinking approach.

Here's how we've tweaked the standard design thinking approach to fit the realities of creating training and performance development programs:

- **The process starts with a problem request instead of with empathize.** In most T&D functions or consulting environments, a request comes to you; you typically aren't sitting around speculating on problems to solve. The request could be someone in the sales function who tells you "Our customer training is torpedoing sales. We need to fix it." Or it could be someone within your organization working on a major change initiative who recognizes that training must be part of change management strategy: "We're rolling out this massive new performance management approach and software tool. We have to train people on the process and the tool." Or you might hear, "Our safety incidents are way up. We obviously need more safety training." You get it: Someone comes to you with a request or a problem that they've already decided should be solved via training.

- **We use the word perspective instead of empathize.** Everything you might read about the empathize step in design thinking books and blogs describes this step as being about getting perspective. So, we opted to simply call it that. Sometimes you can scare people away from a design thinking approach simply because clients distrust it as touchy-feely and solely focused on people's feelings. Feelings are a part of getting perspective, but you're also searching for insights about the learners' realities and work context, along with how they feel about that reality. It also means getting insight into business stakeholders' view of the problem or situation. In effect, your goal is to build 360-degree understanding.

- **Instead of define, we use "refine problem" to describe what to do with a problem statement.** Typically, the stakeholder requesting training comes to you with an initial problem definition. Your job is to help stakeholders refine it based on the perspective-gathering you do. This refinement puts you in position to solve the real problem, not the initial guess of what the problem is. This mirrors what you already do in the analysis stage of instructional design or the "A" in the ADDIE model. It goes beyond the ADDIE model in that it pushes you to ask different questions than you might in an ADDIE approach.

- **The ideate and prototype steps mirror those of traditional design thinking approaches.** The design thinking process kicks into gear when a cross-functional group gathers to brainstorm possible solutions. This group ideally blends people with skills in technology design, visual design, instructional design, and communications with subject matter experts, target learners, and stakeholders. The goal during this step is to create initial prototypes of solutions that the team can quickly test with target learners who provide feedback. When we say prototype, we mean "quick and dirty" renditions of ideas. You're looking for versions that you can easily discard if they aren't right. They can be created with pencil and paper or with minimal digital effort. The goal, truly, is no polish.

- **The next step is iterate.** In traditional design thinking models, there is a testing step that follows iterate. In our framework, we've blown out iterate to show you that it is a process of testing, refining to the point where you can pilot, and then, as needed, refining again. The goal as you refine is to share early and often so your target learners can see and test solutions before you get them so evolved that having to revise them is painful for all involved. A key phase within the iterate stage is piloting the solution. That pilot helps optimize the solution. Skipping a pilot is a bit like choosing a bunch of recipes you've never cooked before and using them for an important dinner party without a trial run on any of them. You'll have some successes—and likely some major misses.
- **The final step is implement.** This step is omitted from traditional design thinking models. The reality with training solutions is that, ultimately, they get implemented. You won't necessarily continuously iterate your learning course or program (which, for example, is what software-as-a-service products do when they are rolling out a new version every six weeks to three months).

Chapters 4 through 9 take you through these steps in much greater depth and describe tools and techniques for executing them.

Four Principles That Matter

T&D professionals are busy, and staying up to date with the latest concepts is an uphill battle. As practitioners ourselves, we're keenly aware of this reality. If you are nervous about starting fresh with an entirely new framework from one you already know and love, then we suggest you focus on the principles that underpin the framework. These principles can fit into a variety of instructional design frameworks and help you produce a better learning experience and better business results. Doing so can give you positive impact on the learner's experience and on business results without incorporating an entirely new framework for doing your work. Number 1 is specific to learning. Number 2 is about humanizing what you do. Number 3 gets to balancing learner needs with business needs. And number 4 is about failing fast to succeed faster.

- **Principle 1.** Recognize learning as a journey. People don't learn from events; they learn from an experience that begins with them noticing a need to learn something and doesn't conclude until they can consistently integrate the learning into their performance. Events don't produce that integration; multi-pronged steps in a learning journey do.
- **Principle 2.** Get perspective. You need to gain perspective from the business (via stakeholders) about the business needs and desired operational results, from learners about what life is really like in their workspace, and from both groups regarding assumed and actual constraints.
- **Principle 3.** Find—and mind—the sweet spot. Recall from chapter 1 that the "sweet spot" is the balance between what the business needs, what the learners need, and what the project constraints are. A project must find that balance and then stay in balance: Don't just get perspective at the design stage, reference that perspective from the business and from learners as you develop and refine your solution. Include stakeholders and learners in early testing as well as late stage testing to ensure you stay inside the sweet spot.
- **Principle 4.** Prototype before you refine. The best solution is typically not the first one you come up with. Be prepared to do quick and early prototypes, get feedback, and refine as you go. You'll end up with a more learner-centric solution (if learners are the ones providing you with the feedback).

We'll reference these principles as we explain tools and concepts throughout the book.

The LXD Framework in Action

Our framework is not intended to be a strictly linear process, though you do eventually have to progress beyond prototyping into development and from developing into implementation. Table 3-1 outlines what this process might look like if it unfolds as the typical project request that a training and development professional might receive. Where iteration is desirable and typical, we've grouped steps together in a single row. We then identified the typical project activities you might execute within those steps of the framework, goals you need to achieve, time to allow from a schedule standpoint, and the tools that can help you as you execute steps.

This chart can also help you visualize how you might incorporate tools and techniques into another instructional design framework. Simply focus on the activities and map them to your current framework. You can then identify tools to use based on the goals you want to achieve. For reference, we've bold-faced common milestones or deliverables that occur within a step.

All of the tools identified in the table are explained in detail in chapters 4 through 9. As you explore those chapters, refer back to this table for context of where the tool might be used within a training design project.

Table 3-1. LXD Framework in Action: Project Plan

Step 1: Respond to Initial Request			
Key Tasks	Your Goals	Time to Allow	Tools to Try
• Schedule and conduct **a kickoff meeting**. • Conduct kickoff meeting with requester. • Map and verify stakeholders.	• Learn what the requester knows and believes about problem to be solved. • Discover initial assumptions about constraints. • Find out who has a stake in solving the presented problem, including learners. • Gain buy-in for perspective gathering.	• 1 day • 60–90 minutes to conduct actual kickoff conversation and begin building blueprint or stakeholder map.	• Strategy blueprint • Stakeholder mapping

Steps 2 and 3: Gain Perspective and Refine Problem			
Key Tasks	Your Goals	Time to Allow	Tools to Try
• Schedule and conduct interviews. • Do observations. • Collect and analyze data. • Create empathy maps with target learners. • Create learner personas. • Create experience map of current state: Identify any magical or miserable moments within it. • If appropriate, produce summary report of findings.	• Obtain perspective from those who have biggest stake in resolving the problem. • Refine the problem based on insight from these varying perspectives. • Clarify what success looks like and how it will be measured.	• 1–3 weeks, depending on availability of stakeholders (including learners). • An alternate approach is to embed these activities within a multi-day design meeting. This reduces quality of analysis but lends speed. Perspective gathering becomes first half-day of meeting.	• Observation • Interviews and focus groups • Stakeholder mapping (making updates after gaining perspective) • Empathy map • Experience map • Learner personas • Strategy blueprint • "How might we . . ." problem reframing

Table 3-1. LXD Framework in Action: Project Plan (cont.)

Steps 4 and 5: Ideate and Prototype			
Key Tasks	Your Goals	Time to Allow	Tools to Try
• Schedule and conduct **a design meeting.** • Build and refine **prototypes.** • Create a **design blueprint** that summarizes instructional goal, learning objectives, and components of each step in the learning journey. • Schedule and conduct post-meeting review of final design blueprint.	• Diverge and then converge ideas that yield optimal solutions. • Fail fast: Test and refine ideas quickly. • Plan out entire learning journey rather than focusing on a single event or tool.	1–4 weeks total time. This includes: • 1 week to plan and prep for design meeting (time may overlap with perspective-gathering activities). • Up to 3 days' time to facilitate the design meeting, depending on size and scope of the project. Duration affected by size and scope of initiative. • 1 to 2 weeks post-meeting, regroup to refine ideas and create summary documentation of design; gain agreement from stakeholders.	• "How might we . . ." problem reframing • Opportunity reframing • Learning journey map • 5-minute think • Learning battle cards • Sketching and storyboarding • Paper or digital prototyping

Step 6: Iterate (Develop and Refine)			
Key Tasks	**Your Goals**	**Time to Allow**	**Tools to Try**
• Create testable versions of your components. • Conduct testing with target learners. Obtain feedback. • Agree on revisions; refine and build next iteration. • Pilot full version of solution. Obtain feedback and identify needed revisions. • Revise and finalize. • Note: Number of iterations depends on size and scope of solution.	• Organize your work into sprints lasting 1-4 weeks. Build your solution out via small iterations to enable frequent feedback. • Involve learners and focus on minding the sweet spot you found by executing earlier steps in the process.	Development varies in length. A single module may take a month to develop, (including review cycles) whereas a lengthy curriculum could take a full year.	• UX testing or user testing grid • Learner personas (as a reminder) • Strategy blueprint (again, as a reminder of plan you created)
Step 7: Implement			
Key Tasks	**Your Goals**	**Time to Allow**	**Tools to Try**
• Execute communication campaign and change campaign. • Schedule and monitor activities outlined within learning journey. • Track metrics; report outcomes.	• Support the journey and ensure all steps get activated, not just the learn step. • Monitor and report metrics. • Execute evaluation plan.	The time varies widely for implementation, from a few weeks to a full year, depending on the scope of the initiative and the metrics being tracked.	• Strategy blueprint (as a reminder) • Implementation plan template

The Design Meeting

Many of the tools we explore—particularly those in chapters 4, 5, 6, and 7—relate to the design of a learning experience. A core element of how we work is to facilitate a design meeting where numerous design decisions get made and initial ideation and prototyping happen. The output of this meeting is a design blueprint, which documents:

- the business need and problem we're solving
- learner personas the solution is focused on
- a description of the learning experience, including the instructional goal and learning objectives, the components that comprise the experience, and initial mockups or prototypes.

This approach may differ from your process, so we wanted to provide a sample design meeting agenda (Table 3-2). We've annotated it so you can see where the traditional elements of instructional design get addressed as we use various design thinking tools and techniques.

This agenda is organized as a one-day meeting. A design meeting like this often results in a small curriculum of three to five training components, such as e-learning courses, instructor-led workshops, reinforcement activities, and job aids. For the purpose of this agenda, we assume we have had an initial conversation with the core stakeholders to better understand the need or request, but that this is our first interaction with target learners and the wider stakeholder team.

Table 3-2. Sample Design Meeting Agenda

Time	Activity	Description
8:30–8:50	Introductions	Each attendee shares their stake in the project and the role they will play throughout. Sometimes we will incorporate a more fun way to get acquainted such as Rory's Story Cubes. Each person rolls a die and then shares a fact about themselves that relates to the icon showing on the die or perhaps a way their view of the project relates to what they see on the story cube.

Time	Activity	Description
8:50–9:30	Refine the need and outcomes	We started a **strategy blueprint** during our initial kickoff conversation with a stakeholder. Here we allow all participants to augment the initial info we gathered. We then have attendees identify those challenges that can be resolved via training versus those that cannot.
9:30–10	Build empathy map	This assumes a single audience. If you anticipate multiple **empathy maps** for multiple audiences, extend the timing here. We often begin the **learner persona** at this stage of the design meeting and finish it as part of the design document. If you were able to do pre-meeting interviews and observations, you can come into meeting with the empathy map started and invite participants to refine it.
10–10:15	Break	
10:15–11	Build experience map	**Experience maps** are a good way for the full team to gain shared understanding of how a job is performed or what a day in the life of the learner really looks like.
11–11:20	Agree on the instructional goal	This is a full-group discussion: what behavior change is expected from the learning experience we are designing? This involves pulling in data from strategy blueprint (challenges section, empathy map, and experience map).
11:20–12:30	Confirm and edit instructional objectives	We may have pre-drafted some suggested objectives, or we may need to brainstorm them based on the newly created instructional goal and information gleaned from mapping activities.
12:30–1:30	Lunch	You can flip things and go to lunch after forming instructional goal. First activity post-lunch becomes creation of instructional objectives.

Table 3-2. Sample Design Meeting Agenda (cont.)

Time	Activity	Description
1:30–2	Align on solution formats' meaning and options, confirm constraints, discuss style	There is a lot going on here in a relatively short amount of time. First, we like to share examples of potential solutions: • to create shared understanding of what we mean by "coaching guide," "web app," or "how-to video," for example • to help warm up the team's creative muscles. Within those examples we include a variety of visual styles to help the team articulate their style preferences. Finally, we confirm what constraints and parameters a solution must be designed within. Are there file size limits? Is data required for completion or scored assessments? Is translation required? Are we really rolling out in six weeks? What specifications do any tech components have to comply with? What kinds of reporting do we need? Who is or is not available to help?
2–2:30	Map the learning journey	While we may have introduced the learning journey earlier in the meeting, this is when we decide which components and activities will be part of each step within the journey. We focus first on the learn step and then frame the other steps to support it. This satisfies the wants of the stakeholders and also helps everyone see exactly what must be supported.
2:30–4:30	Brainstorm (break as needed)	Here you can use a variety of ideation techniques. For a curriculum, we often divide into small groups and assign each group one solution to design.
4:30–5	Share out ideas and conclude the meeting	Unless the full group ideates together, a sharing session allows everyone to weigh in on the solution designs.

Table 3-2 offers an agenda for a one-day design meeting. But what about a multi-day version? The key difference between a one-day version and a multi-day version is the amount of ideation and prototyping you do within the confines of the meeting. In a multi-day version, you may do initial ideation with your client and then schedule a four- to eight-hour timeframe where you work with your team to create the first "sacrificial" ideas for testing. You then reconvene with your client and share or test the ideas with them, doing initial refinements based on their feedback as you do.

This saves a huge amount of time overall and builds momentum quickly. If it's possible to do a multi-day format, we recommend it. However, a word of caution: Having decision makers and target learners in the room together is key to this version's success. There is little point in designing terrific ideas that team members love if decision-makers aren't part of that team. That approach is a recipe for "swoop and poop": an idea gets really far in its evolution only to have a key decision maker who has been nowhere in your process come in and kill the idea.

Work on Your Own

Before reading the rest of this book, take a moment to reflect on the biggest differences between our LXD framework and its four principles versus the process or model you use to design learning experiences or training programs. Ask yourself these questions:

- Which steps and activities are similar to the process or model you typically use?
- Which steps or activities are completely unique to the LXD framework? How might you integrate those aspects into the model you use?
- Of the four principles, which one resonates most with you? Which one would make the biggest impact on the learning experiences you create?

Summary

This chapter explained the LXD framework, which serves as an organizing framework for the next several chapters. It also outlined four principles that underpin the model:

- Principle 1: Recognize learning as a journey.
- Principle 2: Get perspective.
- Principle 3: Find—and mind—the sweet spot.
- Principle 4: Prototype before you refine.

Regardless of whether you adopt the framework, you can incorporate the four principles into your current practices. You can also use Table 3-1 to quickly scan the tools we explain in subsequent chapters.

Section 2 of the book works through each step of the LXD framework, starting with Get Perspective and Refine the Problem. Chapter 4 starts with the problem your stakeholder brings to you, which sets the entire process into motion.

GET PERSPECTIVE AND REFINE THE PROBLEM

Start With the Business Perspective

In This Chapter:
- How to respond to an initial request and inquire about challenges
- Getting to useful descriptions of a problem or opportunity
- Who has a stake in solving the problem?
- The importance of agreeing what success looks like

Typically, those who design and develop a training or performance development solution do it in response to a request. Some common situations that trigger a request for training are:

- **A major change:** change in roles, structures, or processes being the most common. As part of the change rollout, people need communication about and training on the new process, roles, structure, or tool being rolled out.
- **The launch of a product:** salespeople need to learn about the product to sell it; customer support personnel may need to learn about the product to service or support it.
- **Onboarding of new personnel:** people need orientation to a company, a role, or specific tasks within the role.
- **Repeated challenges or mistakes:** quality problems, safety issues, inefficiencies; in each of these instances lack of training is often cited as a culprit. Common complaints include: "People don't know how to follow the process" and "People don't know how to do the job correctly."
- **Communication challenges or interpersonal conflicts:** soft skills have a huge impact on how work gets done. Common requests start with "We need to train people how to manage conflicts better/be more vocal/be more assertive/be more collaborative/work better as a team."

- **Growth goals:** organizations often set financial growth targets that trigger a need for people development so the organization can achieve its targets.

Included with the request or mandate may be specifics related to the format, duration, and timing of a training solution. Your job is to work through that request to refine everyone's understanding of the problem you're really solving. (Note: "problem" may equal a need to respond to an opportunity. Not all "problems" are negative.) Your goal with the get perspective and refine the problem steps is to clarify the problem you are supposed to design a solution for.

This chapter walks you through the process of turning an initial request into a specific description of the challenges you need to resolve, what success looks like, and how success will be measured.

Responding to an Initial Request

As our LXD framework shows (Figure 4-1), the processes of getting perspective and refining the business problem are iterative.

Figure 4-1. The LXD Framework

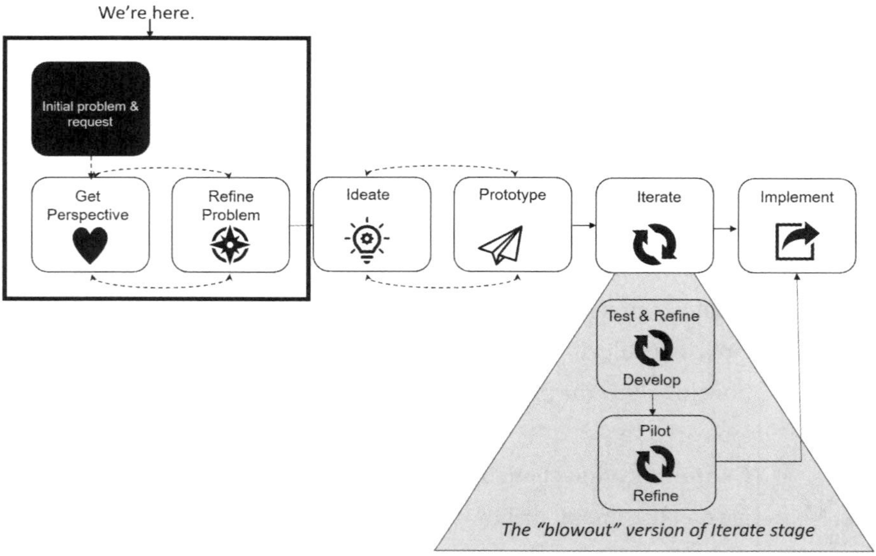

This framework combines a traditional ID approach and design thinking approach.

You start by working with the initial requestor of a solution. Let's look at two example requests:

- **Example 1:** "We need people ramped up faster; we need you to redo our onboarding program."
- **Example 2:** "We're rolling out new leader standards; we need training on feedback and coaching to support those standards. Can you create a one-day workshop on feedback and coaching for managers?"

Both examples suffer from several issues that make them poor problem descriptors:

- **They lack specificity.** You can't tell how big the problem is or where exactly it exists. (All new hires across the company or just a specific segment of them?) You don't have any evidence to support the problem as a problem.
- **They don't quantify the problem or clarify its impact.** How much does this problem cost the organization? What impact is this having on productivity, retention, employee engagement, and so on? What ripple effects does this problem cause elsewhere and for whom? There's not a true description of the problem in either of them; each simply sounds like an assumption of fact.
- **The solution is incorporated into the problem description.** The requester has clearly decided that training is the solution, but a well-formed problem description doesn't include the solution. Perhaps both scenarios could benefit from a training component, but without better problem definition, you'll likely design ineffective training. You will also fail to recognize and address other issues that may be affecting performance. (See Figure 2-1 in chapter 2 for all the factors that contribute to performance.)

You don't have to tell your client that their request is wrong or premature. Instead you can ask questions to better understand the challenges your client is facing. Better understanding helps you partner with the client to design a learning experience that solves those challenges.

This chapter walks you through two tools: stakeholder mapping and strategy blueprints. Let's look at stakeholder mapping first.

Stakeholder Mapping

Remember the "sweet spot" Venn diagram from chapter 1 (Figure 1-1)? The three intersecting pieces represented business needs, learner wants and needs, and constraints.

The definition of what the business needs—or what the problem really is—usually cannot be fully defined by a single person or role in the organization. Multiple perspectives of a problem exist and need to be understood. A stakeholder map can be a quick way to gain insight into all the people or roles affected by a problem.

Figure 4-2 shows a sample stakeholder map for the situation where someone has asked you to revamp the onboarding program so they can get new hires up to speed faster. Let's assume this request came from an HR director within a CPA firm. She's made the request because someone came to her and said new hires need to get ramped up faster. Working with her, you could quickly build a map that looks like Figure 4-2.

Figure 4-2. Stakeholder Map

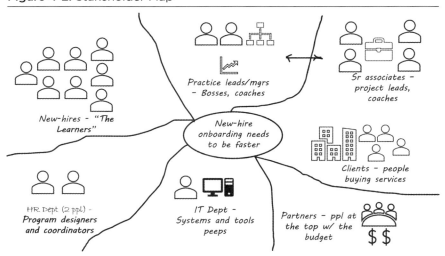

This visualization of the stakeholders associated with a problem helps you and your client understand whose perspective is needed to fully grasp the challenges to be solved with a training solution. You can add arrows to the map to show dependencies. We've shown one here.

To help you identify the stakeholders, ask questions such as:

- Who is funding the project?
- Whose support is essential to you as you design and build a solution? Maintain it?
- Who benefits from the project being implemented?
- Who (or what) could be an obstacle to solving the problem? ("Whats" are often associated with "whos." For example, complex software systems might be associated with the IT function as well as with the partners, who may not want to spend money to buy more current software tools.)

Stakeholder mapping can start as soon as you begin discussing the request. You can expand its usage, if desired, to incorporate key pieces of information that you gather as you go. You can then share updated versions of the map with stakeholders to verify you've captured their perspective and understanding of the challenges you're uncovering. As you get started with perspective gathering among the business stakeholders, look for:

- Dependencies between stakeholders.
- Stakeholders who have influence over other stakeholders. (For example, the partners in our map likely have major influence over the practice managers. Practice managers, in turn, likely have a lot of influence over HR.)
- The most important stakeholders.
- The biggest challenges of each group: What's the same and what's unique? What challenges will a learning experience solve and what challenges relate to other performance factors that are external to your target learners?

Strategy Blueprints

Armed with a map of your stakeholders, you are ready to conduct conversations about challenges, success criteria, and success measures related to the original training request you received. A great tool to help you do this is a strategy blueprint. This tool originated with a user experience (UX) designer named

Jim Kalbach who designed the blueprint to think through the UX needed for digital solutions (Kalbach 2014, 2016). We find it is useful for helping clients think through the learning experiences (LX) they hope to create. It is also useful to help illuminate what challenges a learning experience will not solve. Figure 4-3 contains a blank version of the blueprint.

This tool sets you up to refine the initial problem you were presented by your client. Use the prompts within each box to get perspective from various stakeholders. The tool can help you start to reframe the initial request you received for a training solution into something solvable. It helps you ferret out the specifics and impact of a problem and separate the solution the client may have started with from the real challenges to be solved.

Even better, a strategy blueprint can be a key tool for one of the four principles we introduced in chapter 3, which is to "find and mind the sweet spot" (principle 3). Strategy blueprints can be a reference for a team as well as a North Star for stakeholders. They ensure that everyone stays focused on the challenges that need to be resolved, the aspirations for success, and the guiding principles to which the design of the solution needs to adhere.

Figure 4-3. A Strategy Blueprint

Challenges What problems are you trying to solve? What obstacles must you overcome?			
Aspirations What does success look like? What will people do, say, or perform differently?	**Focus Areas** What is the scope of the solution? What will you focus on for the most impact?	**Guiding Principles** How will you overcome the challenges? What specific mantras will guide teams as they develop the solution?	**Activities** What types of activities solve the problem? What capabilities achieve your aspirations?
		Outcomes What metrics will be used to gauge success? What types of measures will you use?	

Used with permission from Jim Kalbach.

Here's a detailed walk-through of each section of the map. Our approach is to fill in the gray sections of the map first. The focus areas and guiding principles tend to get filled in as we gather learner perspective (chapter 5). The activities portion gets filled in as we ideate and prototype (chapter 7).

With that in mind, let's look at how you might work with stakeholders to complete each section on the blueprint.

Challenges

Start building your blueprint by asking the question, "What problems or challenges are we trying to solve with a learning experience?" Alternately, if you are trying to capitalize on an opportunity you might ask, "To do X (a product launch, a process rollout, or some other initiative), what obstacles to implementation of a successful learning experience do we need to overcome?" The responses you get can help you refine a problem statement. Tips to follow include:

- On your initial go-through, simply let people brainstorm. If you have a large group of participants working on the blueprint, allow each person to share their perception of the top challenge. Don't worry if you hear challenges that are completely unrelated to training or performance development. You want to get those onto the table.

- Collate the challenges you hear; people may express the same challenge in different words. See if you can consolidate similar ideas into a single statement.

- After you allow people to brainstorm responses to your question, have them go back and do two things. First have them rate the challenges in order of priority to solve. Second, have them note which challenges or obstacles are caused by lack of skill or knowledge and which ones are due to other factors. For example, in one session we facilitated to brainstorm challenges related to selling a product, lack of access to buyers was a challenge. This lack of access wasn't caused by lack of skill or knowledge on the part of sales representatives. It was a function of the overall healthcare environment, which restricts sales reps' access to physicians. Training cannot fix this problem, but it is still exceedingly useful for those designing training to know this challenge exists. This knowledge enables them to include information on how to deal with limited access.

- Agree on what you are doing specific to non-training challenges. Then remove or cross off the non-training challenges from your map. Your strategy blueprint is focused on designing a learning experience. Focus areas and guiding principles unrelated to the learning experience won't yield a useful strategy blueprint.

Aspirations

To complete this section of the blueprint, invite people to tell you what success looks like: "If we eliminate or address all the challenges, what will we see and hear in the workplace that shows us we were successful?" Tips to follow include:

- Encourage people to be descriptive. What will people say, do, think, and feel?
- If people cannot agree on what success looks like, go back to challenges and make sure everyone is aligned on what the primary problem is and challenges are.
- If the challenges are many, push people to vote on the top three and focus their aspirations on resolving those.

Outcomes

This is where you document the metrics that are evidence of solving the problem. Push for metrics that already exist. If you're not measuring it now, it's going to be tough to start or to figure out a means for tracking. Ideas for where to pull metrics and data from include:

- **Customer relationship management (CRM) system.** This system will contain contacts, leads, opportunities, and closed won or lost sales. Most CRMs allow filtering of data so you can compare individual salespeople to each other or districts to one another as well as extract reports at specific points in time. If you don't have a CRM, find out how you track sales data and use that instead.

- **Accounting systems.** These systems enable you to pull revenue and expense data and usually filter by service areas, products, and more. The data from an accounting system can be useful for identifying a variety of metrics such as revenue per employee, expense per employee, and net profit.
- **Talent management systems.** These systems may contain salary information by role, tenure, experience levels, and more.
  - **In manufacturing,** you should be able to access safety incident reports or deviation reports.
  - **In service companies** you will likely be able to pull project data that helps you assess profit margins on projects, effort required to perform tasks, roles required, and more.
- **Engagement surveys.** Many companies—large and small—do annual employee surveys as well as periodic pulse checks. You can compare before-and-after scores and data, though many, many things will affect engagement scores. Isolating a change down to one thing can be tough to do.

Focus Areas

As you progress in your project and pull learners into the perspective-gathering process, you are ready to ask the next question on the blueprint: "To address the challenges, achieve our aspirations, and produce the outcomes we specified, where do we most need to focus?" One tip for success:

- Make sure people can link the focus areas they recommend to the aspirations and the challenges. Do the focus areas address the key challenges or obstacles? For example, you may find that a performance issue stems from a process deficiency. In that case, process improvement would need to become a focus area, not just training layered on top of the process shortcoming.

Guiding Principles

What handful of principles should guide the design of the solution you create for learners? Let's imagine that all the associates in the accounting firm referenced in Figure 4-2 are field-based and on the road frequently. They don't always have access to a WiFi signal because of the remote areas they sometimes go to. The principles might be:

- Meet learners where they are (new to experienced).
- Show, don't tell.
- Enable me to find it fast.

Activities

Activities equate to tactics. They are the things you do to solve the problem and achieve the outcomes. They should fit within the focus areas you defined and honor your guiding principles. A single focus area may have multiple activities associated with it.

Putting It Into Action

We've shared the important elements to consider for each part of the strategy blueprint. Now, refer back to the two initial training requests provided at the start of this chapter. Let's look at how you might use the prompts within the strategy blueprint to help refine the problem and clarify what success is going to look like.

Example 1

In example 1, you now have information you can use to better define "ramped up faster" and clarify how business stakeholders want to measure success (Table 4-1).

From those responses, you can begin to flesh out some potential focus areas of a learning experience. One likely focus area is going to be redistribution and leveling out of the onboarding load. Another is likely to be emphasizing the project types that account for 80 percent of the work instead of trying to orient new hires to a wide array of project types in the first year. As you pull in perspective from the learners themselves (chapter 5), you are likely to discover more focus areas and gain insight into guiding principles as well.

You can also flag challenges that likely go beyond what training can solve. In this case it is unwieldy software tools, a statement we've marked with an asterisk in the example to highlight it for you. Going back to Wile's performance model in chapter 2, you should recognize this challenge as a tools problem, not a training problem. Ultimate success in speeding up new hires' capabilities with the software may partially depend on finding better software.

Table 4-1. Example 1: New Onboarding Program

Starter request	We need people ramped up faster; we need you to redo our onboarding program.
Responses to "What challenges do you need to resolve?"	• It takes 18 months to get a new, fresh-out-of-college accountant up to speed and independent on client projects. This is partially because there are so many project types the firm wants people to learn. Some are basic; others are highly complex. • We're investing too much time in ramping up new hires and it's affecting our utilization and billing. • New associates' billable time takes too long to get to the 1,800 hours the firm considers fully productive. • Senior associates who are coaching new associates struggle to hit their own targets because of the ramp-up demands. We're losing billable hours from both groups as a result. • When new associates can't master the basic work quickly (80 percent of what we do) it means senior associates get tied up doing it. That limits availability of senior people to do the complex work (20 percent of what we do). As a result, we lose out on our most profitable work. • There's a large volume of information that's included in current onboarding; it's a lot for a new hire to digest and it's a lot for senior associates to cover with new hires. There are also several unwieldy software systems that are not intuitive to learn.*
Responses to "What does success look like?"	• New associates are successfully executing basic projects within 6 to 9 months after hire. • The onboarding is more focused and manageable. It doesn't take as much time for managers to be part of it. • We aren't turning down the complex projects due to lack of capacity or resources available to do the work. • Our senior people aren't having to work 80+ hour work weeks to bill their target 38 hours per week.
Responses to "What metrics offer evidence of success?"	• Billable hours logged by new associates. • Total hours per week worked by senior associates compared to their billable hours.

Example 2

Example 2 is a bit trickier because lots of things may affect a manager's ability to give timely feedback and appropriate coaching (Table 4-2).

Table 4-2. Example 2: New Performance Management Standards for Leaders

Starter request	We're rolling out new leader standards: We need training on feedback and coaching to support those standards. Can you create a one-day workshop on feedback and coaching for all our managers?
Responses to "What challenges do you need to resolve?"	• We've committed to rolling out new standards in six months' time.* • Within our performance management system, managers are going to be rated on their abilities to deliver effective feedback and to provide appropriate coaching. Their pay increases will be linked to these ratings. • We struggle as a culture to do a good job with either coaching or feedback. It's not done consistently across the organization.* • We want to be a "best place to work" and have competitive advantage in our ability to attract and retain top talent. That requires strong coaching and feedback skills in our managers.
Responses to "What does success look like?"	• Employees feel connected to their managers and engaged in their work.* • Managers are proactive in their coaching and feedback.* • We're seeing less issues escalate to HR.* • Current engagement survey data indicates managers score low in both the feedback and coaching areas by a full 15 points. We currently average 70 points. Low engagement translates to decreased productivity and increased turnover.
Responses to "What metrics offer evidence of success?"	• Engagement survey ratings that average 85. • Turnover percentages decrease by 5 percent across all areas of the company.

In this example, we've asterisked numerous items because the environment itself is likely to be a big factor in performance. Training, by itself, will not make a workplace one where people feel connected and engaged. However, you have something to work with here as you continue to gather additional perspective. You also can invite your stakeholders to vote on the items they think a learning experience is likeliest to resolve. For instance, a training session on techniques that can foster connection might be helpful.

Getting Agreement on Success Measures

In the preceding examples, you started with nebulous requests and gathered insights that have teeth. You went beyond asking about challenges to asking what success looked like and how stakeholders would measure it. Failure to specify aspirations and measures of success at the beginning means you have no means of assessing success in any objective way. That leaves you with the totally subjective method of asking for opinions. You have no scientific way of evaluating whether you solved the problem that the training solution was supposed to solve.

For some great perspective on the criticality of evaluation, we turned to our colleague Dr. Will Thalheimer, a distinguished author, research-to-practice consultant, and learning-evaluation innovator.

Why Learning Evaluation Matters
By Will Thalheimer, PhD

Determining your end goals is paramount as a starting point in developing learning-and-performance solutions. Once you have a clear vision of your outcomes, you can determine what solutions are needed—without the common prejudice of defaulting to training as the sole solution.

If you do determine that a learning initiative is essential in getting to your end-state vision, that's when you need to start considering learning-measurement issues. Indeed, as I have argued for many years, before you determine your learning objectives, you should determine your evaluation objectives. That is, you should first agree on the measures, metrics, and evaluation approaches you will use to measure your outcomes.

This process—starting first with defining evaluation objectives and learning outcomes—is critical, but it is not enough. When thinking learning measurement, you must step back and ask how you can be most effective as a learning professional. One critical part is making informed decisions based on valid evidence. The primary goal of learning evaluation must be getting data that helps you make our most important decisions.

There are three reasons to engage in learning measurement:
- showing the outcomes or benefits
- supporting learners in learning
- improving the learning.

Everything depends on you being able to monitor effectiveness and improve the learning.

Coming full circle then, when you begin the design process, you should outline your evaluation goals in discussions with your stakeholders—considering the cost-benefit tradeoffs required. Get your stakeholders together and ask, "What do we want to target in our learning evaluation?" As you discuss what is possible and the costs and resources required, you can work out a mutually acceptable agreement with your key stakeholders to get the data you need to help you and the organization make its most important decisions about your learning solutions.

(In chapter 11, we discuss how Will's Learning Transfer Evaluation Model fits into this conversation.)

In the two examples we showcase in this chapter—and in the endeavors you do—the client likely can identify some potential metrics that can be tracked. Your job is to partner with the client to probe for specifics associated with those metrics. Let's look at example 1 of the CPA firm whose associates need to onboard more quickly (Table 4-3). The righthand column shows more specific ways to represent the metric. You get to that level of specificity by asking the client, "What metric seems attainable? By when? How can you measure it?

Table 4-3. Success Measures for Example 1

Possible Metrics	Specific Measures to Assess
Billable hours logged by new associates	• Within six months, new associates are averaging 32 hours of billable time. • Within 12 months, new associates are averaging 38 hours of billable time.
Total hours per week worked by senior associates compared to their billable hours	Senior associates who oversee and coach new associates maintain billable targets of 38 hours per week but do not exceed 55 hours per week of total time worked.

Ultimately, the client decides what measures are reasonable to assess. Your job is to facilitate the conversation and ask the client these questions:

- If you consistently hit the metrics you've defined, is this adequate evidence that you've solved your problem?
- If you consistently hit those metrics, is this adequate evidence that you've achieved your aspirations of success? (Aspirations are the qualitative description of what success looks like; metrics are the quantitative evidence that success has been achieved.)

Realistically, you will not always have clients that can articulate metrics or have metrics they can measure. But if the investment in the training solution will be significant, try hard before giving up. No evaluation of your efforts is possible without those metrics.

A Simpler Alternative: "How Might We . . . ?"

Problem reframing is a simple design thinking technique that can be used in conjunction with or as an alternative to a full-blown strategy blueprint. To use this technique, you might start by asking about the challenges that stakeholders need to solve (this equates to the first step of the blueprint model). You can then invite stakeholders to flip those challenges into statements that invite people to reflect on an alternate reality or a vision of the future that involves solutions.

Check out how this reframing statement can look when used with example 1 in this chapter (Table 4-4). Each challenge gets reframed as a question that begins with "How might we . . . ?" After all challenges get reframed in this way, you can invite stakeholders to nominate the top two or three to be the focus of the learning experience (if indeed the chosen statements are solvable via training).

Once the team votes on refined statements they want to proceed with, pull learners into the conversation and start ideating possible new realities. (Ideation is covered in chapter 7.)

Table 4-4. Using "How Might We . . ." in Example 1

Challenge	Problem Reframing
It takes too long to ramp up new associates; 18 months' time on average.	"How might we design a solution that lets new hires become productive in six months' time?" (Note: Six months' time may not be realistic but ideating on possibilities can create innovation.)
Tenured associates get pulled for basic project tasks and bottlenecks form around the complex projects.	How might we eliminate bottlenecks with senior associates and complex work?

Work on Your Own

Use these two activities to practice what you've learned in this chapter.

Activity 1: Use a Strategy Blueprint

Try taking a blank strategy blueprint (appendix 2) and assessing a training solution you created against that blueprint. See how well you can:

- Articulate the challenges the solution was intended to solve from both the stakeholder's standpoint and the learner's standpoint.
- Describe what success was supposed to look like from the stakeholder's perspective and the learner's perspective.
- Identify metrics you could have used to measure success.
- Recognize the focus areas.
- State the guiding principles that defined the experience you created.
- Summarize the activities and map them to the guiding principles and the focus areas.

Perhaps you can fully map the learner experience using this framework—or perhaps you will realize some gaps. If you can map your solution to the strategy blueprint, good for you! If not, recognize the framework as a useful means to more fully outline the learning experience that can drive the results you want to obtain or help you get clarity on the results expected of a learning experience you're tasked with designing.

Activity 2: "How Might We . . . ?"

Consider your company's onboarding—and some of the challenges connected with how it's done. Brainstorm those challenges and then reframe them as "How might we . . . " statements.

Consider how doing so helps you and others shift from focusing on problems to imagining possible future states.

Summary

Clear descriptions of the problem to be solved by a learning solution help focus the project team and enable the team to define relevant success metrics. This is the first step toward finding the sweet spot and sticking to principle 2: get perspective. The next step toward the sweet spot is gathering the learner's perspective, which we discuss in the next chapter.

⑤ Pull in the Learner

In This Chapter:
- Learning perspective gathering versus traditional needs analysis
- Tactics and tools for gathering learner perspective
- How to know which tool to use
- Refining the problem with learner perspective

The last chapter focused on understanding the business perspective. That's important—it's one of the three components necessary to identifying the sweet spot. Once you have that perspective, however, it is time to balance it with input from the target audience. In this chapter we show you how to collect the perspective of your learners to better understand the learning landscape and get information that is critical to:

- Continue refining the problem.
- Draft an instructional goal and objectives.
- Decide what content supports those objectives.
- Select the best format for the learning solution.
- Plan a learning journey that gets results.

When collecting learners' perspectives, your goal is to gain as complete a perspective as possible and continue to identify constraints (which we address in chapter 6). For training and performance development projects, learner perspective often includes:

- who the learner is (demographics, role, experience)
- what their day-to-day realities are (thoughts and feelings, environment, tasks, tools)
- when, why, and how they perform the task of interest
- the magical and miserable parts of their job, as a whole, and the task of interest, in particular.

Figure 5-1. The LXD Framework

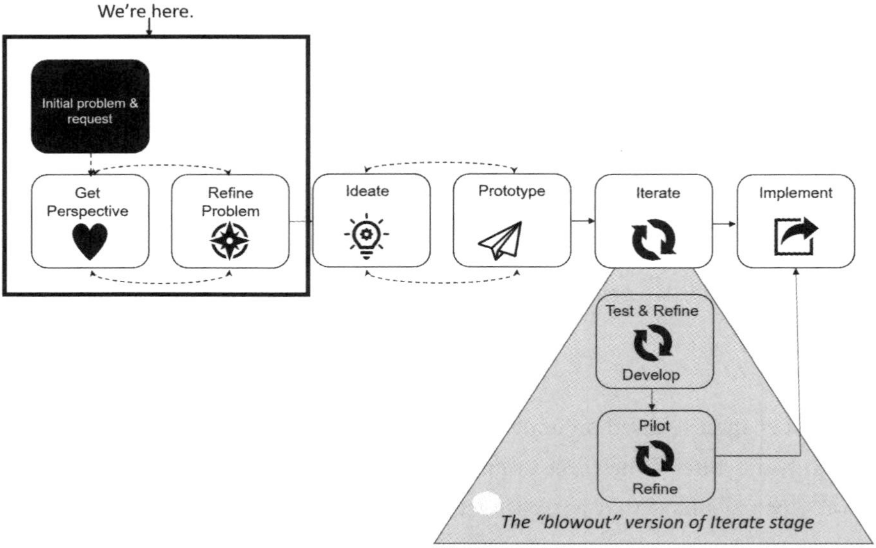

In addition to getting perspective from your business stakeholders, you need to gather the perspective of the learner.

Ideally, you uncover this information in a way that all the project stakeholders are able to hear it. A shared understanding of the learner's realities means you don't have to be the sole advocate for the learner—instead, the whole room aligns on what the right solution is, and why.

If you're accustomed to using ADDIE, SAM, or another design model, you may wonder how this step is unique from the analysis step. It's a good question—there are many similarities to a needs analysis or audience analysis, but also some key distinctions.

In a traditional needs analysis, you focus on identifying gaps between current and desired performance. You're essentially asking, "What is [role] doing? What should [role] be doing? And how do we move them from the current to the future state?"

In contrast, gaining learner perspective requires insight into the learner's tasks, interactions, tools, thoughts, feelings, and environment to uncover obstacles inherent in their daily realities that may be hidden in plain sight. You want to know things like, "What are you thinking about when you do [task]? What motivates you to do [task]? What challenges or obstacles do you face while doing [task]? What does the environment look like where you do [task]?" Hearing this info from learners often highlights constraints, non-training issues, additional training topics not previously considered, conflicts between use case and format, or other ways to minimize miserable moments in the learning journey.

This approach also goes beyond most audience analysis, which focuses heavily on demographics, background and experience, and preferences. These are a part of the learner perspective, but you'll need more information to uncover how this solution about this topic will be consumed and applied on the job.

Tactics and Tools for Getting Learner Perspective

In this chapter we'll describe each of these tools:

- observations
- interviews and focus groups
- empathy maps
- experience maps
- personas.

These are the primary tools in our toolbox. We mix and match them based on the project and its constraints. We typically use a few of them on every project; we seldom use all of them. Most are tools we use before or during a design meeting, which was described in chapter 3.

A quick web search for "empathy map," "experience map," or "persona" yields a variety of templates and examples. We've included templates we prefer for applying these tools to training and performance development.

Observations

If the project budget allows, nothing can replace seeing target learners perform the task of interest in their own work environment. In an ideal world, this approach would be the rule, not the exception. One could argue that it is presumptuous or even condescending to design training for a task you have not observed "in the wild." Learners place trust in us to create training that is relevant, accurate, and well-suited for its intended purpose. One way to generate buy-in and trust is to spend a few hours showing genuine interest in what those things mean.

Unlike a needs or task analysis, however, don't fix your attention on the step-by-step process of what they are doing; instead, absorb the contextual details such as:

- What tools are they using, and how user-friendly are the tools?
- How much does the task rely on rote memorization and past experience versus job aids and tools?
- What interactions or communication are required to complete the task?
- What distractions are going on around them, and how do those impact their performance?
- Where is the task most likely to break down or encounter errors?
- How conducive is the environment to performing the task?

An observation checklist of questions like these will help you to notice those things once you're on-site. You can find an example of an observation guide in appendix 3.

Here are two tips for conducting your observation. First, it's hard to know what data will be most meaningful, especially at the beginning of an observation. Spend time in advance thinking about how you're going to use observation data; that should help hone the number of things you need to pay attention to. For example, if you know the scope of your project doesn't include the possibility of a new software system, observing the usability of that system may be a waste of time you could have spent otherwise. However, if you think creating software job aids may be a potential outcome, watching the system in action and recording a few screenshots may be very valuable.

Second, when you observe an individual, often it is their off-hand comments that provide glimpses into potential opportuni-ties and serve as the spark for valuable discussion during the design meeting. Make sure your checklist allows room to document these remarks! For example, we observed an employee who was describing her onboarding experience and commented, "We have to take courses on [company] university, but they all look the same—by the time

I finish one, I don't know what course I just took." We shared this comment at the design meeting to socialize the idea of doing something to set apart the onboarding modules from other required courses.

After you have completed the observation, go back through your data with the original performance problem or desired outcome in mind, asking yourself, "So what?" Decide what could inform your design versus what merely informed your understanding of the performance landscape. Group your observations into categories to help stakeholders understand how the factors impact the design.

Get Real: Virtual Observations

We get it: Observations can be expensive when they require travel, especially if all you need is a couple hours on-site. But with the technologies available today, consider how you might get creative. While it may not be a substitute for the in-person experience, there are benefits to taking the virtual approach.

When it comes to software training, we have often not been able to get our own user access to the system in question. Instead, we've had good luck doing observations via webinar, during which registered users share their screen and perform key tasks in the system. Seeing the user interface in action is better than receiving static screenshots. If you're permitted to record the webinar, it serves as a valuable reference for the rest of the project.

A couple years ago, we went to do observations at a college campus to learn how administrators (exemplary performers) completed a complex process involving student data. Because of the number of different roles involved and the amount of time over which the process unfolded, it was not possible to directly observe all the tasks live. However, the campus team devised a creative solution: They created a video of the process for us to watch. They went to the office of each participant in the process and had them model what they do at that step. While it was probably a bit contrived for some of the participants, it was an invaluable resource for us. Not only did we still see contextual details (such as which steps were paper-and-pencil versus electronic, which software systems were used for each step, which job aids were referred to along the way) it was also a way to share the process with team members who weren't able to go on-site, and was a source that we referenced repeatedly throughout development.

With mobile phones and optical head-mounted display devices readily available, video is easier than ever to record, which could help make lengthy, remote, or dangerous tasks more accessible for observation.

Interviews and Focus Groups

Interviews are a quick, informative tactic that can be used in isolation as well as before or after an observation. A sample interview guide is included in appendix 4. Here are a few best practices we've discovered:

- **Number of people.** An interview is a one-on-one affair in which you can expect to hear lengthy responses based on that person's individual experience. As you add more people, it becomes a focus group, in which you can expect to hear shorter responses that highlight similarities and differences in each individual's experience. Both formats are valuable; you may want to decide which will work best once you've had a chance to decide what types of questions you want to ask. Regardless of how many respondents are involved, there should be two members of your team there: one to transcribe the responses and one to facilitate. The facilitator should be free to ask follow-up questions or modify the line of questioning as necessary to yield the best data without having to worry about capturing each response. If you cannot get two members of your team to participate (or you are a one-person band), then record the interviews so you can transcribe the interview after you finish.

- **Use in tandem with other methods.** Of course you can do a series of interviews in isolation, but they can be more powerful when used before or after observations or focus groups. Much like reading a book before going to see the movie can inform the latter experience, an interview leading up to observation of an unfamiliar task can help prepare you for what you'll see and help focus your attention on the most important factors. For example, our first observation of a mining facility was loud, hot, (and fascinating!) with lots of things to capture our attention. It was very helpful to look at site photos and talk to stakeholders before the visit. An interview after an observation provides an opportunity to ask targeted follow-up questions about what you saw (or think you saw).

- **Combine qualitative and quantitative responses.** When asking for open-ended responses, try not to "prime the pump" by asking questions like, "Tell me why this task is difficult." And balance open-ended questions with quantitative responses, which allow you to directly rank or compare responses. Narrative responses uncover valuable insight, but they are not easily compared apples-to-apples. For example, instead of asking respondents what they think is most important for a new employee to learn, present a list of potential topics and ask respondents to rate the importance of each topic on a scale of one to five. Those ratings could provide a clearer picture of which topics should be included for new employee onboarding.

- **Manage your time.** Prioritize in advance the questions that you must get responses for so that if (or when) the interview gets off track, you walk away with the most important responses. You can also give yourself time markers to ensure you leave enough time for critical questions. For example, in a 30-minute interview with three sections (background questions, task-related questions, and training preferences) you might allot 10 minutes for each section. Then, the clock will help you know when it's time to move on.

You may notice that we highlighted interviews and focus groups but not surveys. When it comes to gathering perspective, surveys can be counterproductive. Not only are good survey questions difficult to write, but they also force respondents to provide quantitative answers to questions generated based on what you think you know. They rarely provide a good forum for learning the rest of the story, and often that's exactly what you're looking for. For example, consider the following survey question:

"How often do you refer to the user guide for help when using the Very Software Program?"

Imagine you asked that question because there are three known support resources. You want to gauge which one is being used most often so you can discontinue the ineffective ones and create more resources like the ones people prefer. The survey results for this question indicated low usage of the user guide. What the survey can't tell you that you could learn during an interview might include facts like:

- Most respondents wouldn't be able to find a copy of the user guide even if you paid them.
- They would like to refer to the user guide more, but it's organized so poorly, they can't find what they're looking for.
- The user guide is organized well, but the entries are all written in hard-to-understand technical language.
- The user guide was the go-to resource until Cathy on the fourth floor created a just-in-time job aid that most administrators post above their computers. You didn't know about that job aid, so it wasn't mentioned in the survey.

When it comes to perspective gathering, surveys are more useful after a few initial interviews to confirm your own understanding of the problems and opportunities. For example, we recently created a survey that was designed to confirm whether there were regional preferences about training content and formats. We had already done interviews and a focus group to understand the learners' general realities, so we drafted a survey that was well-informed by that initial information, then sent it for review by target learners on the core team before the survey was published.

Empathy Maps

ssed for time? Empathy maps are a great way to paint an illuminating land-
the learner's environment in a relatively short amount of time. An em-
covers aspects of the learner's thoughts, feelings, environment,
motivators, and challenges (Figure 5-2). Appendix 5 offers a
is information represents the types of contextual details
tion, plus an intentional inquiry about the learner's
a task. That broad perspective is especially helpful if

you are unfamiliar with the role of your learner, as T&D professionals can be as external consultants or as part of a separate internal department. It's also critical for challenging stakeholders' assumptions about a role or highlighting aspects they were unaware of. For these reasons it is one of our primary sources when we construct a learner persona, which we'll discuss next.

Figure 5-2. An Empathy Map Template

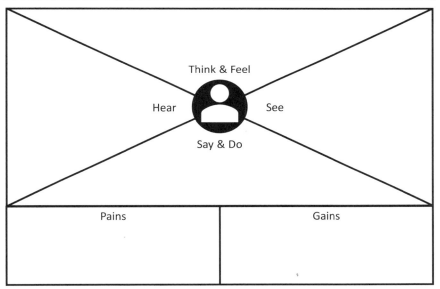

You can populate sections in any order, though we like to fill in pains and gains last, because at that point learners have many aspects of the role in mind. To fill each section of the map, ask learners to answer these questions:

- What are you **thinking and feeling** about X? (X can be whatever it is you want people to learn or know about, or it can be their current reality. The prompt is going to depend on what your project is. In an onboarding project it might be, "What did you think and feel as you started your new job?" In a sales project, it might be, "When you are trying to position a brand-new product, what do you think about? How do you feel?")

- What do you **see** while you do X? (For example, what is your environment like, what devices and tools are you using, or who do you interact with on a daily basis?)
- What do you **hear** from others as you do X or apply knowledge of X in their jobs? (For example, what messages do you receive from the supervisor, peers, or customers? What do you hear people talking about?)
- What do you **say and do** in relation to X? (For example, what tasks are you performing and what conversations are you having? Who are you talking to?)
- What are your **pain points** in attempting to do the task or applying knowledge? (For example, what challenges do you encounter, and what makes it difficult or unappealing?)
- What are the **motivators** for doing the task or applying knowledge successfully? (For example, what do you stand to gain by doing it well?)

Here are some process pointers on how to generate an optimal empathy map:

- **Talk to real learners.** Too often, we have arrived at a design meeting to find that the "target learners" we were promised are actually the target learners' supervisors or former target learners who have been promoted out of that role. That's a red flag! Sometimes, yes, these people have performed the role in recent memory, but other times it's been five years or more since they were doing the day-to-day activities of that role. The problem is, no one in the room has the ability to tell the difference between what is or is not accurate information, meaning you won't know if you're getting closer or farther from the right solution.
- **Provide context.** Depending on the scope of the project, you may want to understand a role at the most general level. However, for more targeted projects, you will get more useful responses by narrowing the context to a specific time period or task area. Here are three examples that become more specific as project scope becomes more targeted:

○ For a broad sales training curriculum, a generic role-based empathy map will work well. Provide context for the empathy map by asking sales reps to consider their holistic role.

○ If you want insight into the mentality of a brand-new hire, specify: "As you were going through the onboarding process for new sales reps . . . " (Note: if the person is too far removed from being a new sales rep, they aren't your target. A sales rep with several years' experience likely has forgotten most of what onboarding was like.)

○ For specific software training, specify: "As a sales rep working in XYZ application . . . "

- **Tailor your prompt questions.** Many of the online templates for empathy maps have generic prompt questions baked into the image. To get the most insightful responses, ask prompt questions that include relevant context. For example, if you are focused on creating an improved onboarding process, include that context in your questions: "As you were going through the onboarding process, what did you think about and what were some of your concerns?" and "As you were going through the onboarding process, what challenges or obstacles did you encounter?"

- **Do it live.** We have learned that an empathy map is not something you can send as a worksheet for learners to fill out. The responses we received were generic, carefully worded for political correctness, and fewer than we would have gotten in person. Plus, it was clear that respondents didn't fully understand the types of answers we were looking for in some quadrants. We needed to facilitate the process so we could provide context and guidance on responses and push back when responses seemed unrealistic or unclear. If you cannot do the map in person, you can do it virtually, but do it voice-to-voice. Ideally, show your screen so people can see what's being typed as a map gets populated.

- **Ask learners to generate each response on a separate sticky note.**
  We usually facilitate an empathy map at the front of a room, so we
  create a large map on flip chart paper. You're welcome to write in
  responses with flipchart marker, but we prefer using sticky notes,
  for several reasons:
    - When learners have time to generate ideas individually, it
      engages everyone equally. You don't have one strong voice in
      the room dominating the responses.
    - Once sticky notes are on the map, we move them around to
      group similar ideas, so duplicated ideas become visualized in
      clusters.
    - Occasionally, a response is posted that fits better into another
      category—for example, learners post key quotes in "think
      and feel" that fit better in "say and do," merely because they
      haven't been asked about that section yet. In that case, it's
      great to be able to capture those ideas and still move them
      around easily.
- **Use different colors to represent sub-audiences.** During the initial audience discussion, it's not uncommon for multiple "versions"
  of a role to surface—for example, sales rep hires who have industry
  experience versus those who don't. Empathy maps are a great way
  to visualize whether or not these are really separate audiences or
  not. Consider using three colors of marker or sticky notes as you fill
  in the map: Color A represents characteristics both audiences have
  in common. Use color B for characteristics specific to the first audience, and color C for characteristics specific to the second audience.
  Brainstorm responses as a group, and have a single person transcribe participants' responses to questions so group members can
  agree or disagree with whether characteristics apply to both groups.

Journey Maps or Experience Maps

For journey or experience map tools, we look to our friends in the marketing industry, who have been doing customer experience mapping for years. There are a range of ways people define the terms *journey map* and *experience map,* and in fact the terms are often used interchangeably. A key distinction is that some visualization maps document tasks a person is doing; other maps show the experience a person is having while they do something. Both tools are valuable for gathering learner perspective, so for the purpose of this description, we will use "experience map" as an umbrella term for both.

Experience maps capture the details of sequential events or tasks. You can use experience maps to gain perspective about what and how a learner performs in a particular context. For example, this tool can capture "a day in the life of an equipment operator," which can be broken down into tasks, each with their unique challenges.

An example of the template we often use is shown in Table 5-1. A blank template can be found in appendix 6. While we have most often used experience maps as a data collection framework to inform the design of a learning experience, you'll find other examples formatted into a visualization tool to illustrate the highs and lows of an experience.

Table 5-1. An Experience Map Template

Major Steps	Complete Start of Shift Checklist	Respond to Incoming Calls	Respond to Guest Inquiries	Other Details
Actions				
Timing and Frequency				
Thoughts and Feelings				
Challenges, Distractions, or Mistakes				
What Sets Apart a Star Performer				

To facilitate an experience map like the one in Table 5-1, start by generating the tasks across the top. You can decide how granular you want the tasks to be based on what you want out of the map. For example, if you're more interested in empathizing and gaining perspective, you might take a "day in the life" approach. If you need more insight into the tasks themselves, highlight more granular steps of a process or key behaviors within a competency such as the "sales process" or "core leadership behaviors." From there, it's a matter of working through each row.

- **Actions.** What are the steps needed to complete this task?
- **Timing and frequency.** How often is this performed, and what prompts it? (For example, when a new hire accepts an offer, or about once a month.)
- **Thoughts and Feelings.** What is the emotion associated with this task, and what is going through employees' heads as they perform the task? Is there anything magical or miserable about the step?
- **Common challenges, distractions, and mistakes.** Where do performers typically make errors? What gets in the way of perfect performance?
- **What Sets apart a star performer.** What are the best people doing that ensures success?

As you populate the map with responses, group common themes to help process the ideas that are coming up. Responses often provide valuable insight into content you didn't know you needed and other implications for the design:

- Information in the *actions* row can often be translated directly into instructional objectives. For example, when gathering perspective about a sales process, we used an experience map to document what that process entails. Many of those "actions" were skills that a new sales rep would need to execute the sales process.
- Information about the *timing and frequency* of tasks, combined with information about performers' thoughts and feelings, is similar to the information collected via Difficulty, Importance, Frequency (DIF) analysis, a common task analysis model. (An example is shown in appendix 7.) Mundane tasks that people perform every

day may need a simple job aid. But critically important tasks workers only perform periodically or tasks that cause anxiety warrant in-depth explanation and practice.

- As learners discuss common *mistakes*, you get important cues about content to include. We often hear examples that make for great scenarios in training solutions.
- Information about what sets apart *star performers* is often synonymous with "unwritten steps of the process." For example, when we ask what successful sales reps are doing during a sales call, we might hear, "Well, they're logging notes about each and every conversation with the customer. They then reference these notes before their next conversation." Aha! Now as we teach new sales reps the sales process, we can set the expectation that the task "complete the sales call" actually has three steps: "review call notes," "perform the sales call," and "log call notes."

Learner Personas

A learner persona is a fictional character who embodies the traits of the learner group and conveys the thoughts and emotions of that group. Personas help you synthesize the information you have collected about the target audience, and establish a way to keep the learner front and center for you and the rest of the project team as you make design decisions. A project may have a single persona or may need several, depending on how many unique learner segments you have.

From the training and performance development perspective, personas help inform the content and format of the learning experience. They do this by providing insight into the demographics and mindset of the learner, as well as the context and use case of how they're going to interact with the eventual training solution. For our training designs, we build a persona by culling data from interviews, focus groups, observations, or empathy mapping with target learners. Sometimes we can assemble a draft persona before we kick off a design meeting; other times we need to build it as part of a design meeting. (Our decision is based on how much perspective-gathering we were able to do prior to the design meeting.) Here are steps for building a persona:

1. Build a basic profile that contains demographic information as well as information about the person's job context. This is often the easiest information to get. Find out your learners' basic details: education level, how they got into the role, past experience, tenure within organization, age range, and typical work environment.

2. Use interviews, observation, or an empathy mapping activity to discover what your learners think and feel, see, hear, and do, as well as their pain points and motivators.

3. Use the design meeting—as well as pre-meeting interviews—to help you learn the things that should feed into your personas:
   - How will they access training?
   - How much time can they commit to training?
   - How soon after initial training will they actually apply their new knowledge or skill on the job?
   - Is this content they'll need to come back to again and again?
   - What level of background knowledge can be assumed?
   - What will make this learning experience most relevant to them?
   - How can pain points they encounter be minimized; how can motivators be leveraged?

   As you find data that answers these or other design-related questions, pull them into a list to be included in the persona. While you're knee-deep in the data, decide what "key quote" sums up this learner. A key quote helps personify the learner and encapsulates their needs into a single statement. It should come fairly easily to you; some-times there's a perfect quote in the "Say and Do" section of the empathy map; sometimes it's an amalgam of a couple key themes. It may be a particularly pithy comment a target learner makes during the design meeting.

4. Once you have the contents of the persona, decide the best way to format it. There's no single right way to create a persona. At a minimum, we like for a persona to include five categories of information:

- personal profile info (name, personal background, experience)
- key quote (one phrase that summarizes what a solution needs to do for them)
- realities (facts about the work environment)
- challenges
- motivators.

Those categories usually accommodate the most important factors; you might also decide to include other information that's meaningful to that particular project, such as "values" or "technology."

5. Finally, choose a picture to represent the persona. If you opt to include an image, we recommend you involve your full project team in choosing the face of the persona. Doing so has three benefits:
   - it's a low-stress team-building activity
   - it forces team members to read the full persona at least once during the project
   - after choosing the face of the persona, team members are more invested in the identity of that person.

Be aware that people are prone to drawing conclusions about a person based on a photo; a particular hairstyle or outfit may not resonate with stakeholders' mental image of the learner. Also, sometimes organizations want to showcase diversity by having diverse images. This backfires with personas. If your demographic is largely white men (as is the case with U.S. farmers, for example), don't feature a black female image in the persona, as that's not accurately representing your actual learner. (Note: using an image can be a sensitive decision. Our decision to include them is made on a case-by-case basis; to avoid unintentional bias we are starting to shift away from them.)

Figure 5-3. Example of a Simple Learner Persona

"This is completely new to me. I have a lot to learn before I am confident talking about the new product line."

Personal Profile

Tasha is 29; she is constantly on-the-go between her job and her family.

- She's been a sales rep for three years and sells mostly ABC products.
- She knows her market and is learning more each day about the product portfolio. She prides herself on hitting or exceeding her goals.
- She doesn't know much about the new product line, but she is interested in learning the technology.
- She is excited by the recent technological advances.

Challenges

- The new product line has a reputation for being complicated and time-consuming to learn.
- She cannot talk about the value of the new products like she can for ABC products.
- Her customers may have limited opportunities to use the new product line.
- She has to be prepared for the sales conversation to go lots of directions, sometimes with deep technical detail.

Daily Realities

- Tasha relies on her laptop, tablet, or phone for her day-to-day activities.
- She often works from her car or customer locations.
- She is busy selling lots of ABC products, so getting her full attention may be a challenge.

Earlier we mentioned that more than one persona might be needed for a project. How will you know? How do you know what constitutes one persona versus what should be broken into multiple personas? Our guideline is that if a group's characteristics impact the way the content or format is designed, that group warrants its own persona. See the following Get Real segment for examples.

Get Real: Persona Proliferation

When you start creating personas for your learners, you may immediately start to doubt whether you're creating the right personas or not. Here are a couple of examples of when we included multiple personas, when we didn't, and why.

Stick to one: We were creating sales process training for around 170 new-hire sales reps, all in the U.S. The client team shared that there are really three kinds of new hires:

- brand-new grads with no industry or sales experience
- external hires with industry and sales experience
- internal hires with sales experience in a different business line.

So the question is: Do we have three personas? The first thing we asked was what percentage of the full group did each sector represent? (We don't want to create a unique persona that represents a tiny fraction of the audience and misguides design decisions.) In this case, the split was about 20, 40, and 40 percent. So the next step was to create an empathy map of a new hire's first couple months in the field. We chose to focus on the second profile, because that was the background of the learner in the room. As we created the empathy map, we asked others in the group to listen for any characteristics that did not seem to represent the other two profiles. There weren't any. The big differences were in product knowledge, which was not in the scope of this sales training; if product training was included, then including a new-to-industry persona would have been much more important.

Double up: We were designing a product launch event for around 100 global attendees. Having worked with this client before, we knew that regional differences existed, but that training should not be region-specific. What did emerge was that the attendees represented a mix of roles: some were sales reps or sales managers who would ultimately sell the product or manage reps who would. But many of the attendees were marketing managers. They were there to learn about the product and to prepare to train the sales reps in their region. Upon returning home, the marketing managers would present pieces of the original launch training plus any supplemental materials they decided to create. Applying our "content-format" guideline:

- Content is not heavily impacted, as marketing managers need to learn the same product details as the reps.
- However, format is impacted, because materials will need to be easily replicated by marketing managers to present the training in their regions.

In this case, we decided it was best to create a persona for each learner type.

Creating the persona is interesting and fun. But remember that the purpose of a persona is to personify the learner throughout the project. Unless a representative learner is actively involved in each step of the project (a luxury we've rarely had), it can be a challenge to keep the persona alive throughout the project. Here are a few ideas to get you thinking about what might work best for your team.

- **Create a persona wall:** Choose a space in your office where you can post personas for all your active projects.
- **Include the persona in content collection documents:** As you begin working with subject matter experts during development, include the persona directly in the worksheets or slide decks you provide. This reminds them of who they're ultimately speaking to and can help them filter what is and isn't relevant for that learner.
- **Post the persona in the project team meeting space:** Does your team meet in the same conference room? Give the persona a literal seat at the table. Or at least put them on the wall as a constant reminder of who ultimately has to live with what you are building.

Choosing Your Toolkit

You have many tools to choose from, and each one requires time—from you, from the target learners, and from the project's stakeholders. While some large projects may benefit from using all these tools, that would be overkill for other projects. Here are a few tips to help you decide what's best for your project:

- **Observations.** Have you ever seen the task in question done before? Have you seen the target learner in their "natural habitat?" If the answers to those questions are "no," an observation can be extremely useful. If access to an environment or learner is restricted for legitimate reasons (such as regulatory or proprietary reasons) replace an observation with interviews or experience maps.

- **Interviews and focus groups.** If you know you will not have access to learners for the design meeting, interviews or focus groups beforehand are critical. These can be executed virtually if you cannot meet in person. Ideally, use a web camera if you cannot meet live. You can include questions you would have asked to create an empathy or experience map.

- **Empathy maps.** If you have learners in a room, create an empathy map. This approach is a quick way to gather a broad perspective of the learners' realities. If you do not have learners in the room, then don't bother with the empathy mapping. You cannot create an empathy map with stand-ins for learners. That's speculation, not empathy mapping.

- **Experience maps.** Like empathy maps, experience maps should only be created with learners in the room. This tool is helpful for painting a picture of what a day in the life looks like for a particular role, or to dig into the detailed tasks of a particular process. Mapping a day in the life is especially worthwhile if you couldn't do an observation.

- **Learner personas.** We advocate for creating a learner persona for every project. However, you can only create one if you've done prior perspective-gathering activities with target learners. By assembling a persona, you are confirming that you understand the audience well enough to create something usable and effective for their work environment.

Figure 5-4 is a decision tree that illustrates these considerations. Every project has unique factors, so this decision tree is not presented as a hard-and-fast rule, but rather a way to start thinking about what tools will best support the perspective gathering process for your project.

Figure 5-4. Decision Tree for Perspective-Gathering Tools

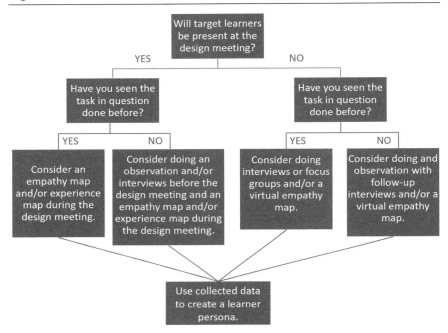

The tools and tactics in this chapter are a great place to start, but they are not an exhaustive list. There are many techniques for facilitating perspective gathering, and we continue to see new ideas all the time. If you're looking for fresh ideas, the Stanford University d.school is a great place to start. It offers lots of information and resources on Its website, including the "Bootleg" PDF with a set of tools and methods for perspective gathering, ideation, and more (visit it at dschool.stanford.edu/resources/design-thinking-bootleg).

Using Perspective to Help Refine the Business Problem

Remember that to verify and refine the business problem, you need to get perspective from learners in addition to business stakeholders. The learner perspective helps your initial picture from stakeholders come into focus. Table 5-2 shows the onboarding example from chapter 4, with the learner perspective added.

Table 5-2. Example 1: New Onboarding Program

Starter request: We need people ramped up faster; we need you to redo our onboarding program.

Question	Stakeholder Perspective	Learner Perspective
"What are the current challenges with the onboarding process?"	• It takes 18 months to get a new, fresh-out-of-college accountant up to speed and independent on client projects. This is partially because there are so many project types the firm wants people to learn. Some are basic; others are highly complex. • We're investing too much time in ramping up new hires and it's affecting our utilization and our billing. • New associates' billable time takes too long to get to the 1,800 hours the firm considers fully productive. • Senior associates who are coaching new associates struggle to hit their own targets because of the ramp-up demands. We're losing billable hours from both groups as a result. • When new associates can't master the basic work quickly (80 percent of what we do) it means senior associates get tied up doing it. That limits availability of senior people to do the complex work (20 percent of what we do). As a result, we lose out on our most profitable work. • There's a large volume of information that's included in current onboarding; it's a lot for a new hire to digest and it's a lot for senior associates to cover with new hires. There are also several unwieldy software systems that are not intuitive to learn.*	• "After the formal onboarding, I still wasn't sure what my day-to-day job would look like. It was really high-level. I didn't work independently on a project until two months in." • "I know senior associates are busy, and their time is very valuable. I try not to bother them with little questions, but then tasks sometimes take me twice as long." • "Once I started doing billable work, it was hard to gain traction because each project was very different. It would have been nice to do the same type of project a few times to immediately apply what I learned." • "It's not just the work that is challenging; each project has a different team, and they don't all do things the same way." • "I've been here a year and I'm still figuring out how to use the [software system]. You basically just have to get to a point where it works for you, and hope that's good enough for other folks using your data."

Table 5-2. Example 1: New Onboarding Program (cont.)

Question	Stakeholder Perspective	Learner Perspective
"What does success look like?"	• New associates are successfully executing basic projects within six to nine months after hire. • The onboarding is more focused and manageable. It doesn't take as much time for managers to be part of it. • We aren't turning down the complex projects due to lack of capacity or resources available to do the work. • Our senior people aren't having to work 80+ hour work weeks to bill their target 38 hours per week.	• "I want to feel like I'm making a valued contribution instead of just feeling like dead weight." • "It would have been nice to feel good at one thing instead of feeling bad at everything." • "I understand the senior associates are busy; tell me who you want me to go to with questions."

Hearing this perspective directly from the learners is eye-opening for you as well as the business stakeholders. For example:

- You can hear the frustration in their voices. They want to be successful faster even more than the business does. On one hand, this is great: revising the onboarding program will be a win-win. On the other hand, it's revealing—new hires have been feeling undervalued and not set up for success. This can lead to high turnover if the business doesn't remedy the issue.

- Similarly, they recognize that senior associates are an expensive resource to go to with questions, but they don't currently have an alternative. The new onboarding program should consider who the best resource is.

- They also echo the idea of starting with one type of common project; trying to learn everything means they aren't gaining proficiency with anything.

- Finally, they underscored the fact that the software system is not user friendly. The learner's comment about "hoping it's good enough" after a year of using it should serve as a major wake-up call to the stakeholders.

This information helps clarify the role of a training solution versus the need for accessible support resources and usable tools, and begins to define what the scope of the training should be.

Work on Your Own

Imagine you are designing a learning experience for people in your role. Acting as both the facilitator and the learner, create an empathy map for yourself.

- Tailor the empathy map prompt questions from this chapter to your role, and write down your responses to each prompt. (You don't have to use sticky notes; you can create a bulleted list or spreadsheet if you prefer.)
- After you complete all the sections of the map, practice debriefing the responses out loud, calling out those that might impact the learner experience design.

Use the data from the empathy map to populate a persona, making sure to include personal profile info, a key quote, work-place realities, challenges, and motivators. Remember, this persona will represent you as the learner while the learning experience is designed and developed. What would you want the project team to know to ensure a relevant, engaging, and effective experience?

Summary

You can begin to see why design thinking is described as an iterative process: It does not proceed in a rigidly linear fashion. That's why finding and minding the sweet spot is a mindset and not a step in the process. Maintaining a balance of business needs, learner perspective, and project constraints is an evolving pursuit rather than a straightforward equation.

⑥ Verify Constraints As You Go

In This Chapter:
- The five categories of constraints
- Questions to ask about constraints

In chapters 4 and 5 we explained how to gather perspective from the business stakeholders and learners to better clarify the problem. This chapter identifies constraints you need to attend to while gathering that perspective. The stakeholder map introduced in chapter 4 can be a useful tool here as well. The individuals on it are all ones who may help you identify constraints or check assumptions about constraints.

Every interview or on-site observation you do helps you identify potential constraints. Within a design meeting, a running list may be maintained as the meeting progresses. Sometimes we draw the "sweet spot" Venn diagram shown in Figure 1-1 on a wall or flip chart and use sticky notes to document constraints as we go and to highlight ones we need to check out before assuming them to be true.

Your primary tools for identifying and verifying constraints, whether as part of the design meeting or as part of the pre-workshop data gathering, are observation, listening skills, and questioning skills. You should ask questions of all the stakeholders who influence or are affected by the problem you have defined. These stakeholders may be learners, the business sponsor, managers, IT people, or customers. If you do observations prior to a design session, you should note the constraints you can see within the environment. If you do interviews, you should listen for cues as people describe their experiences, feelings, and what they say, do, and hear as they go about their jobs.

The Five Categories of Constraints

Constraints are a tricky thing. Sometimes they are real; other times they are assumed but not actually real. As much as possible, you want to list the known constraints before you start ideating solutions, though a few end up being challenged as you ideate and come up with solutions. Budgets can magically appear if solutions are compelling enough. Timelines can get elongated if a perceived solution seems valuable enough.

Most constraints fall within one of five categories:

- budget
- time and timeline
- technology
- people
- environment.

Note that "environment" is a massive category that includes regulations, compliance requirements, processes, economic climate, and more. You can revisit the Wile model in chapter 2 for elaboration on all the components related to environment.

Let's look at how you can evaluate the validity of each potential constraint and questions you can ask to confirm how much of a constraint some of these items are.

Budget

The degree to which budget is a constraint can change as understanding of the problem and the potential impact of a solution emerges. Avoid assuming the budget you start with is the budget you must live with. Identifying your budget at the start of a project is reasonable, but as information unfolds you may be able to justify a bigger one (or perhaps a smaller one). Your job is to continue probing as new data emerges during your interviews, observations, and design meeting about the impact of the problem, what might be required to solve it, and what solving it can mean for the business.

Your initial budget allocation usually depends on four factors:

- **Where the problem resides organizationally** (sales versus manufacturing, for example, or client-facing versus internal). Some functional areas have more dollars and resources allocated to training endeavors than others. Those functions that generate cash for a company typically get more budget than ones that don't. This does not mean you have no hope of increasing or gaining a budget unless you are sales or marketing; it does mean that the next item becomes very critical for you to be able to quantify.

- **The expected impact to the organization for solving the problem.** Budgets typically link to the perceived cost of the problem or positive financial impact of a successful solution. If you can quantify the cost of the problem you're trying to solve—and the potential cash generation or cash savings of solving it—then you can often justify a request to increase a budget if a bigger one is required to fully or efficiently solve the problem.

- **How the dollars got decided.** In other words, sometimes budgets are created with minimal thought behind them or minimal knowledge of what a solution might cost. In such cases, budgets are often placeholders that project sponsors are willing to refine after more information is gathered. Here again, being able to explain the impact of a problem or potential solution as well as potential costs for solving it serves as justification. This links to the next item.

- **The sponsor of the project.** If you have a highly engaged sponsor who can influence others, then you can eliminate or reduce a budget constraint with proper justification. Conversely, if you do not have a sponsor at all, have a disengaged sponsor, or have a sponsor with little to no influence over budget dollars, then any budget constraints that exist at the beginning of your project are likely to remain a constraint for the duration of the project. (And if you have no real project sponsor within the organization, you likely shouldn't bother doing the project.)

You should not just assume the budget is the budget. Instead, ask these questions of your stakeholder, your boss, or whomever decided on the budget to clarify constraints:

- How was the budget determined? What factors influenced it?
- What impact does return on investment have on this budget? If you can quantify significant savings or financial opportunity, how might that influence an ability to increase the budget?
- Who allocated the budget? (If it was not your stakeholder, ask your stakeholder what influence they have on the budget giver. If it's zero, then you likely have a bonafide constraint that you won't be able to change.)

Time

As you prepare to ideate solutions, consider what constraints are created by the calendar time in which a solution must be built. You also must identify the hours people have to support the project during that timeline. Both hours and calendar time are common constraints.

The constraints your client claims are true regarding hours that can be expended and calendar time available may be preference or opinion more than fact. Your job is to figure out which it is. Obviously, you want to avoid ideating solutions that the team cannot produce in the hours or calendar time available. Be aware, though, that you don't just probe once and accept the answer as final. As the impact of a problem or the requirements needed to produce the desired solution emerge, decisions about truths related to hours people have available and calendar time in which something needs to get done often change.

Here are two cues that indicate when time and timeline will not change:

- **Solution delivery is linked to an event that is already fixed in time.** A common example of this is an annual meeting or a sales meeting. That meeting date was selected months in advance; its date is not going to change. If a solution must roll out in conjunction with a pre-planned event, then you have a constraint you must work within. You must factor in the hard delivery date as you ideate possible solutions.

- **Failure or delay in implementing a solution puts a function or an organization at high risk.** If there is a huge organizational pain point that is costing a company a lot of money or keeping it from generating income, you will face pressure to move fast. In such cases, good enough and faster are preferred over perfect. This focus should factor into the kinds of solutions you ideate.

Here are three common cues that indicate time could change or be renegotiated:

- **People made uninformed commitments.** Sometimes timeline is driven by a rash promise on the part of a key executive or sponsor who made a commitment before understanding what might be involved in creating the solution. If you can see that estimates of effort or calendar time required were decided without enough information to inform the decision, use information you've gathered to help renegotiate the time constraint.

- **The problem or the opportunity's scope or its impact on the business is far greater than originally described.** To ideate optimal solutions requires you to have the ability to expand your thinking. Needs emerged that you were unaware of when you started your project.

- **You discover that the originally requested solution will not work.** (Remember, your client likely proposed a solution to you as part of the initial request.) As you gathered perspective from learners, you learned facts about the learner's workflow or work environment that negate use of whatever solution was originally proposed. That could mean that time and timeline need to be adjusted.

Similar to budget constraints, you shouldn't assume that the initial time request is set in stone. Instead, ask these questions to clarify time constraints:

- What informed the timeline you've provided to me? What flexibility is there to the timeline? (Hint: If it is not a specific event that your project has to align with, then chances are time is not the fixed constraint someone may be telling you it is, as we've mentioned already.)

- What assumptions did you make when setting the timeline? (Your goal here is to determine if any flawed assumptions drove the decisions on dates. If the assumptions are flawed, dates may become flexible.)
- What matters most: time, quality, or budget? If you had to increase budget to stay within the timeline, is that possible to do? What about if you have to make quality sacrifices?

Technology

Technology is often a major constraint. The reasons for it being a constraint, though, can differ. If a solution requires technology as part of it (such as any type of online solution delivery), here are common constraints you should inquire about. You may pose your questions to several individuals, depending on your project and where it resides. You will want to find out who your IT contact is within the organization or for the project. That individual is likely your starting point, though you may be directed from there to talk with others in the organization. If any type of digital asset is a possible component of a learning experience we are designing, we always request the presence of someone from IT at the design meeting itself—at least for an hour's time.

When you pose questions to your IT contact, they can likely direct you to the best person to answer your questions about:

- **A company's LMS.** Per ATD's 2019 report, *Is the LMS Dead?*, it is not dead and is instead alive and thriving. According to the respondents associated with the report, it also delivers a very bad user experience. If your solution must reside on an existing LMS, you have a constraint to factor into your solution design. Learners will have to go through the company LMS to get to whatever solution you might craft. That affects learner experience; you need to think about how you will optimize it.
- **Devices for consumption of content.** If you want to do something mobile (because your perspective-gathering activities clued you in on learners' need for a mobile solution) you have work to do in figuring out what devices and operating systems to support—and

what the company will not support. You will also have to figure out the testing constraints you need to consider. How many devices will you test on? How will you collect testing feedback? Who can be part of testing?

- **Analytics and reports.** The ability to assess how well a solution delivers results depends on the company's ability to gather metrics. What metrics need to be tracked from the training itself? LMSs largely only track completion of online training and little else. What constraints will you have on your ability to gather the data you might need?
- **Communication with learners.** This item can seem odd to include in the technology category, but technology is typically used to help you communicate messages. As you think about the learning journey—and the need to help prepare people for the learning experience—how will you communicate with learners? What constraints do you need to consider in methods, tools, and access?
- **Implementation and maintenance.** Often people focus heavily on creation of solutions and fail to consider what's required to implement effectively and to maintain over time. What constraints do you need to consider about the company's ability to implement the solution well? What personnel are required to support implementation and maintenance? What budget exists to support implementation and maintenance?
- **Security and IT.** What level of security does the solution require? Is data storage allowed? If so, where? What internal resources exist to support digital solution development? Maintenance? Hosting? What data privacy issues must be considered and addressed as part of solution design? Does the company IT function need to be included in ideation and prototyping?
- **Cost.** There are some technologies that big companies can easily embrace that a small company says "no way" to supporting because of either cost or resources required. In those instances, technology can be labeled off-limits or restricted to a basic, rapid-authoring

product. This constraint links to budget, but since budgets are often associated with design and development and not with ongoing maintenance, this can get missed.

Questions to ask to help you begin to unearth technology constraints include:

- What technology and tools are already approved for use in the development and delivery of learning solutions?
- Is housing the solution outside the LMS negotiable?
- If use of the LMS is not negotiable, what features and tools are enabled on the LMS?
- Are new tools and technologies allowed? If so, what's the protocol for getting approval?
- Who is the appropriate IT contact to involve?
- What technical specifications regarding devices, security, browsers, and operating systems does any solution need to comply with?
- Do you support use of APIs (application program interfaces)?
- Is it possible to use an API to create a single sign-on experience for learners? If so, how much does single sign-on matter to usage? (This is likely something you can test as part of your prototyping process. Let your target learners tell you this one.)

If clients don't know answers to the preceding questions, do not immediately assume your solution cannot use technology that differs from the norm. Probe and see if you can locate IT support resources who can work with you. If you assume you can only use certain tools (such as Articulate Storyline) and that the solution must reside within an LMS, your solution may not be optimized for a learner's workflow or environment.

People

People constraints can involve either learners or the people creating, rolling out, and maintaining the learning experience. Two key ones to start with are: Who must be involved? Whose availability might be an issue?

These are two big questions you want answers to before you ideate and prototype. On the design and development side, failing to include someone who has the power to reject the team's proposal (we call this the "swoop and poop") after you've crafted and gotten excited about a design is a mistake. On the learner side, attempting to roll out a major training initiative at a time when no one has time to focus on it is a second mistake. Ideating a solution that depends on the involvement of someone whose time is extremely limited is a recipe for headaches as well. If a specific person's expertise is needed—and there is no alternative to that person—you must understand and plan for that constraint as part of ideating and prototyping.

Other constraints you need to consider related to people include:

- **Skills available within your team members.** For example, you may have an amazing idea you want to explore that includes use of virtual reality (VR). If no team members have this skill—and no budget exists for outsourcing VR—then this becomes a constraint. You can't ideate solutions that use technologies you don't have the skills to use.

- **Constraints of individual team members' time.** This is both a people issue and a time issue. People's time is the constraint. If one or more members of your team have limited time to devote to designing or development solutions, you have to factor that into your ideation.

- **People's time to participate in perspective-gathering or design efforts.** If you cannot bring learners to the design meeting, for example, you have to think of creative ways (such as 15-minute one-on-one interviews or an email interview) to get perspective from them. If they cannot physically join you at a meeting, but they could participate remotely, you have to work around that constraint.

Environment

Where and how will your solution be used? What, if any, regulatory requirements govern its design or usage? Cues on environmental constraints come from perspective gathering. You won't know about workflow issues, workplace surroundings, compliance requirements, or schedule and time availability issues if you haven't gathered perspective from your learners. What you learn related to environment (what they see, hear, do, and experience as they do their job) has a major impact on design decisions. For example, if an environment is:

- **Loud** or filled with people, ideating solutions that involve use of sound must factor that environment in.
- **Global**, solutions may need to factor in the need for translation or cultural contexts.
- **"On-the-go"** or field-based where employees do not sit at a desk, your solution should consider delivery format.
- **Sales-based** or customer-service based with short call windows, your solution should reflect that reality with examples and practices matching what your learners see, hear, and need to do on a typical sales or service call.

Get Real: Verifying Constraints

We did a project with a nonprofit that desperately wanted to create a game-based solution. They also had thoughts about creating a responsive solution that could be used on laptops, tablets, and phones with the device of choice being the laptop.

We did several on-site visits to the location where people worked and interviewed the target learners, most of whom ranged from 17–22 years old. The combination of on-site visits, coupled with some one-on-one interviews, helped us quickly learn these things related to environment as well as technology:

- Most did not like games or spend much time playing them (defying stereotypes about the demographic).
- Data plans were a huge concern; people in this age group had limited data plans. They would not download things that would blow up their monthly usage.
- There was a single desktop computer available for training in most facilities. The device of choice for these learners was their phones.
- Users had no organizational email address, so we couldn't assume an ability to send things via email or have them log into a system.

All these factors—and more—influenced our eventual recommendations and what we ideated as a team.

Work on Your Own

Think about a recent or current project you have. Use appendix 8 to consider the constraints you have identified in each of the categories. Then see if you are assuming these are constraints or if you have verified them. If you haven't verified them, see if you can identify who might help you do so.

Summary

You don't want to waste anyone's time designing solutions that won't work for learners, the business, or within the organization's constraints. Operating within constraints is a key component of finding and minding the sweet spot. Doing your due diligence as you get perspective from learners and stakeholders sets up you to have a useful ideation and prototyping session, which we tackle next in section 3.

SECTION 3
IDEATE, PROTOTYPE, AND ITERATE

7 Ideate and Prototype

In This Chapter:

- How to ideate
- Prototyping what you ideate
- Iteration checkpoint: test the prototype

In chapters 4 and 5 we explained how to gather perspective from the business and your learners, and then in chapter 6 we outlined typical constraints you need to verify and tactics for doing so. This chapter assumes you're ready to start brainstorming and designing possible solutions (Figure 7-1).

Figure 7-1. The LXD Framework

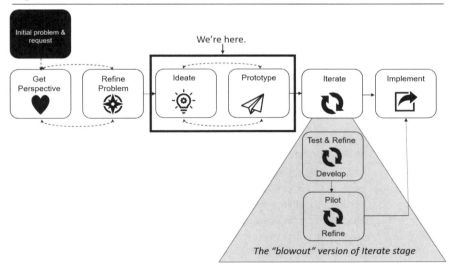

How to Come Up With Great Ideas

What's your favorite go-to training technique or solution? Do you always do a workshop? An e-learning course? Drag and drop activities within an e-learning course? A PDF reference guide? In other words, any time someone asks for training do you use the exact same instructional strategies or delivery methods? The answer here should be "no." Even if you are a consultant who deals with similar problems frequently, the learners you are designing for have unique differences in their environments. Tailor your solutions to the constraints, the perspectives, and the problem you're trying to solve.

Inputs for Ideating

Before you begin ideating solutions, make sure the team has:

- Access to the problem you've refined. Make sure the challenges you're resolving via a training solution are available and everyone understands them.
- Success metrics you want the solution to produce. Again, make sure everyone understands these metrics.
- The instructional goal of the solution and the performance objectives your solution needs to achieve. What performance are you driving to?

Table 7-1 gives you a realistic example, which we'll use throughout the chapter to illustrate proper ways to ideate and prototype.

Table 7-1. Sample Description, Success Metrics, and Instructional Goal

Problem description	PharmaCo has struggled to efficiently and effectively ramp up sales reps on its past five launches. Market penetration has taken twice as long to achieve as was projected. The current approach brings reps in for a two-day sales meeting. At this meeting, marketers deliver product overviews and sales messaging; medical personnel outline clinical trial data and label information. Reps then do role plays. Survey feedback on training workshops is positive, but post-meeting sales don't match expectations. Observations of sales calls show that reps aren't effectively presenting sales messages. PharmaCo has 10 launches planned in the next two years. If reps cannot achieve selling proficiency quickly, these launches will not meet sales and market penetration targets.

Success Metrics	• Market penetration meets or exceeds defined targets. • As evidenced via observation, 95 percent of sales reps can consistently position a new PharmaCo product or indication within 30 days of a product launch meeting. • Six months after launch, territories are within 5 percent of their sales goal targets for a new product. Twelve months after launch they are at target or exceeding it.
Instructional goal	Sales reps competently and appropriately position PharmaCo products with healthcare professionals and achieve their stated sales call objectives.

Other items you want to have on hand include:

- **Learner personas** you are designing your solution for.
- **Experience maps.** The maps you have depend on the problem you are solving. For the fictitious problem we've listed in Table 7-1, you might want a map that shows a sales call flow, so your team understands the context in which a sales rep sells. You might also want a map of the current learning journey (not the one you'll create but the one that has been true in the past). They should match your problem and your learners.
- **Description of constraints.** You don't want to brainstorm unworkable solutions. If you have a $5 thousand budget, you don't want to ideate a $100 thousand solution. If you must design a solution that requires translation, you need to be aware of that constraint as you make decisions on graphics, audio, and text.

Hopefully you have noticed that these items combine to help you fully represent that "sweet spot" you are to continually be minding. The organization's perspective is represented as part of the problem statement. The learner's perspective comes via the persona and experience maps. The constraints list is exactly that—the representation of project or environmental constraints.

Who Ideates?

Ideally, your design team is diverse. It can include the project sponsor, content experts (such as marketers and medical or regulatory staff in our fictionalized instance), IT, various designers (such as graphic artists, instructional designers, e-learning developers, or writers), and—ideally—a couple of learners or people who have very recently been in the learner's role. See the Get Real story on the power of a cross-functional team.

Get Real: Cross-Functional Design Teams Have Superpowers

We were fortunate enough to support NxStage in designing and developing a solution for helping patients and caregivers become proficient in doing in-home hemodialysis, and a solution that helps nurses effectively train patients and caregivers. NxStage's project lead fully embraced a design thinking approach. She knew multiple perspectives were critical to getting to the right solution for patients, caregivers, and the nurses who support them.

The attendees of the design meeting included two patients who used NxStage's dialysis system, nurses who trained patients, the VP of sales for NxStage, the head of IT for NxStage, and the director of clinical education. From our team we included several people with different backgrounds including instructional design, software engineering, sales, and project management.

We broke these people into small teams and had them either map out the experience of a patient going through dialysis training in a center or map the experience of a nurse doing the training. Both maps, coupled with personas we generated by doing empathy mapping of each role (nurse, patient, caregiver) were crucial to ideating the best solution.

Check out chapter 14 to learn more about this project.

How Do You Ideate?

There is no one right way to ideate solutions. Here are tips that can help to get creativity flowing.

First, start with your personas and experience maps. If you produced these items before your design day, start by reviewing them. Otherwise, begin by creating them. With these perspective-gathering tools, inspect them to:

- **Highlight the key factors you see on the maps.** What stands out? What seems like a critical clue about what's needed or what won't work at all? What constraints are embedded?

- **Locate the miserable and opportunities to be magical.** Spend time thinking through the journey or the persona's empathy map and where "miserable moments" or pain points are. Focus on how you can eliminate the miserable or maximize anything that's magical. Those are areas of big or common wins.

Figure 7-2 shows a persona associated with the problem statement in Table 7-1. This is a persona of the sales reps that undergo PharmaCo's launch training. We shaded the text we saw as important to our ideation. The information within the persona was gleaned from an empathy mapping exercise as well as one-on-one interviews with sales reps.

Figure 7-2. Learner Personas Highlighted for Ideation

"Show me how to use info within a sales call. Give me reinforcement so I can build confidence."

Sales Call Realities
- Calls range in length from 30 seconds to four minutes for a standard call to seven to 15 minutes for a lunch & learn event.
- Lunch events are hard-earned; many times people are primarily interested in free food.
- Figuring out how to incorporate new messaging into that tight call window is often the hardest part of transferring training to the job.

Personal Profile

Susie is 44; she has one daughter and is constantly on the go between her job and her daughter's activities.

She's been a sales rep for 10 years and has experience in several therapeutic areas. She's a seasoned pro and prides herself on hitting or exceeding goals while staying compliant. She doesn't want to be the one to lose respect with an HCP.

Challenges
- Getting it all done in a day.
- Figuring out how to incorporate "new" messaging into existing ones and staying within a 30-second call length.
- Building confidence after formal training on new messaging, product releases, clinical trial info, and so on.

Values
- Having solutions to sell HCPs
- Being a credible voice to HCPs
- Working for a company whose reputation is solid
- Hitting her goals and maximizing income

A Day in Her Life

Days are long. She's up a 6 a.m. The word day starts at 7:30; it may end up around 10 p.m. when she wraps up emails or inputting notes into Salesforce.

Her territory is large; she spends the bulk of her day driving or standing in hallways waiting to see a doc. The total contact time she may have across 12 physicians (a typical call day) may only be 30 minutes.

Figure 7-2. Learner Personas Highlighted for Ideation (cont.)

Technology Realities

Susie is a utilitarian user of technology and not super tech-savvy. Ninety percent of her time she works from her iPad. Her phone use is limited. She doesn't play computer games or video games. Her social media use is limited to Facebook.

She relies on her tablet to display sales enablement pieces during conversations with docs.

She also still leaves behind a lot of print-based materials; some HCPs use tablets and laptops to search for info. Others rely on those print pieces or reprints of journal articles, studies, and so on.

> One tactic to help with ideating solutions is to highlight key insights from a persona. Those insights can be the frame for ideating a single solution or an entire learning journey.

The empathy map associated with this persona highlights some miserable moments for the rep that we need the solution to address (Figure 7-3). Specifically:

- The amount of information they must absorb in a launch meeting is overwhelming.
- The information doesn't align with their sales call flow or show how to use in a sales call.
- There's no reinforcement: you either get it in the launch meeting or you are struggling on your own afterward.

Figure 7-3. Empathy Map Highlighted for Ideation

Think?

"How am I going to place new indications?"

"What's right for the patient?"

"How am I going to fit this new message into my call time?"

Feel?

Anxious and unconfident:

"I don't know enough."

"It's not clear to me how this fits. What if I say the wrong thing in the doc's office?"

Excited:

"Will this enable me to cover more indications and sell more scripts?"

Overwhelmed:

"I thought I understood this . . . but now I don't think I do."

See or Hear?

From docs:

"It works the same as everything else."

"I prescribe your competitor. Works fine, and I don't see why I should switch."

"I don't prescribe any new drug for the first two years it's on the market. I want to wait and see how it does."

From other reps regarding training:

"That was a total waste of time."

"What just happened? . . . I'm not sure I got it."

Do?

Sell on value if the product is innovative or different. Sell on reputation and organization reputation if rep can't really differentiate between their product and competitor products.

Focus on what they *can* say, not what they can't.

Avoid selling a product if they don't understand it; rely on what they know and feel comfortable selling. Revert back to old habits if attempts at selling in new ways don't immediately pay off.

Pain/Challenges

Time it takes to really learn new stuff and time it takes to get *comfortable* with new messaging tools and content.

Nerves: Ride-alongs can be intimidating.

Lack of clarity on how to insert new messages into calls.

Motivators

Get more scripts; earn more money! Gaining interest from docs; getting doc to try a drug on a patient.

Peer-to-peer interaction and story-sharing.

Ride-alongs—an incentive to prepare.

An empathy map offers cues to miserable moments. (An experience or journey map can do so as well.)

Invite people to tell "learner stories" and then map a learning journey that supports those stories. As people craft experience maps of the current state of things, they can often derive stories of what they want to be true as the learner interacts with the training. Document the stories you want to be true for learners and that will help them have a magical (relevant and useful) learning experience.

In our sales rep example, the experience of the current training can lead to stories such as these:

- Sales reps see how the product sales messages can fit into their sales call windows.
- Sales reps easily and quickly find product information on their iPads.
- Sales reps see how adding this product to their portfolio of products to sell makes it easier to hit their goals.
- Sales reps feel supported by their sales managers.
- The learning experience fits into the flow of the sales reps' day.
- Sales reps have ample practice opportunities and get feedback that verifies where they are on track and where they need to adjust.

Table 7-2 pulls together information from the empathy map and the persona to show you the linkage to the learner stories we created.

Table 7-2. Empathy Map + Persona = Learner Stories

Empathy Map Key Points	Persona Key Points	Led to These Learner Stories
Thought: "How am I going to fit this new message into my sales call windows?"	A challenge for the persona: figuring out how to fit new messaging into tight call windows is the hardest part of transferring training into job.	Sales reps see how the product sales messages can fit into their sales call windows.

Empathy Map Key Points	Persona Key Points	Led to These Learner Stories
Feel: Overwhelmed—"I thought I understood, but now that training is over, I'm not so sure."	A challenge for the persona: Building confidence after formal training.	Sales reps have ample practice opportunities and get feedback that verifies when they are on track and when they need to adjust.
Gain: Selling more prescriptions and the incentive to be prepared for ride-alongs. Pain: Nerves of ride-alongs.	Motivated by selling more prescriptions and maximizing earnings. Reps want to be a credible voice to HCPs.	Sales reps feel supported by their sales managers. Sales reps see how adding this product to their portfolio of products to sell makes it easier to hit their goals.
iPads are what reps use throughout their day		
Pain: Nerves of ride-alongs.	"She relies on her tablet to display sales enablement pieces during sales calls."	Sales reps easily and quickly find product information on their iPads.
n/a (This final item actually came from discussion about daily realities and sales call flow mapping that we coupled with empathy mapping).	Days start early and end late. There is a lot of drive time; time in front of doctors may only be 30 minutes total out of an 8- to 10-hour day.	The learning experience fits into the flow of the sales reps' day.

You can then invite people in your design meeting to brainstorm things that make those stories come true. You can take each stage of your journey individually and invite people to think about what needs to happen to progress learners across the journey to the point of competence. Figure 7-4 shows the journey we came up with for PharmaCo.

Figure 7-4. PharmaCo Learning Journey

Sharon's Learning Journey

Values hitting her goals and maximizing income.	"Show me how to use info within a sales call. Give me reinforcement so I can build confidence."		Struggles to build confidence after formal training.		
Notice	**Commit**	**Learn & Practice**	**Repeat & Elaborate**	**Reflect & Explore**	**Sustain Long-term**
Launch communication campaign: "How to win more scripts"	Ensure training descriptions are focused on how to use new messaging during sales calls	Video demos: how to integrate product information into 30-sec, 2-min, 4-min, and 7-min calls	Video coaching tool for feedback on practice sales presentations Podcasts to listen to during drive time	Provide opportunities to share out success stories Coaching guide for Sales Manager during ride-alongs	Integrate into develop-ment plans

A learning journey that solves the problem of sales reps not getting enough practice and contextual examples of what good looks like.

Bring or show some inspiration. Whether you are mapping an entire journey or focusing on a single solution within the journey, inspiration helps people imagine what's possible. Non-designers can get nervous about not knowing what's possible. So, armed with your constraints, start by brainstorming every kind of solution that might be possible. To make that easier, give people inspiration to get them started. For example, we've used Learning Battle cards that contain dozens of ideas for solutions (see Figure 7-5). You can also bring props, such as game-making supplies or apps, websites, books, or images that you've found.

Try getting things started by having the group brainstorm words that the solution might evoke. We've given people "mood boards" to get them thinking about what a solution looks or feels like. Even if you do intend to do an e-learning course produced via a rapid authoring tool, pushing yourself to find inspiration from outside the e-learning world can help you craft more creative ideas for that e-learning experience.

Figure 7-5. Learning Battle Cards

Learning Battle cards can be useful for sparking ideas for learning solutions that go beyond a typical workshop or e-learning course. You can also assemble a Pinterest-style board that includes links to apps, websites, games, podcasts, or other courses to help spark ideas and motivation.

Split people up and allow for divergence before convergence. In design thinking, the amount of ideas often get bigger before they get smaller again. If you are gathering varying perspectives, you will see that you start to get divergence of ideas and perspectives. Allowing people to brainstorm possible solutions in small groups (or even as individuals) enables you to expand your thought pool before converging it back to land on a final solution. By letting people brainstorm within smaller groups you get the benefit of diverging ideas. Bringing them back to the big group allows people to find ways to converge those various ideas.

Tables 7-3 and 7-4 shift away from our PharmaCo example to showcase two techniques for doing this type of brainstorming and divergent/convergent thinking for new-hire training.

Table 7-3. Five-Minute Think

Use this ideation technique to get small groups focused and brainstorming possible ideas quickly. This allows people to diverge—brainstorm a wide array of ideas—and then converge back and select the best option. This technique works best when you can split a big team into smaller ones for the activity. Teams of two to three people work best.

First Minute: Target and Task

Define your goal as precisely as you can.

Example: "We want to come up with a ramp-up technique for new hires that makes it easier for them to be productive within their first 30 days on the job."

Minutes 2 and 3: Explore and Expand

For two minutes, explore ideas. Here are three examples from the original new hire onboarding problem we introduced in chapter 3:

- What if we narrowed the role of a new hire at first and focused on getting them really good at a single project type?
- Could we set up a four-week boot camp that simulates a typical project? The entire four weeks would immerse them in that single "client" experience and they'd learn tools and techniques by doing the simulation?
- Could we break up the first four weeks into one-week assignments with week one being a shadow, week two being a simulation, week three being a review of worked examples, and week four being an on-the-job assignment?

Minutes 4 and 5: Contract and Conclude

You have several ideas and concepts. Compare these to what your teammates got. Do any of them resonate with the team? Are you seeing themes or patterns?

Example: Home in and immerse. The examples from minutes 2+3 all center on the idea of immersion and focus: depth in one area rather than breadth in another.

Share Out

After you finish the five-minute think, each team should share out its ideas and its conclusion. The larger group can then converge on a single idea or a couple of ideas.

Follow the rules of improvisation and say "yes, and . . ." When you are ideating, you do not want to dismiss ideas quickly. Instead you want to allow for exploration. You might start by inviting people to identify the idea that seems the most outlandish or different and then have a small group work on prototyping something that uses that idea. You can then test the prototypes and figure out how you might refine them.

Table 7-4. Fill-in-the-Blank Opportunity Reframing

Use this ideation technique to help you generate design assumptions and questions about a specified problem and solution.

Part 1: Fill-in-the-blank with the problem and your potential solution *(Insert stakeholder or learner)* needs a way to *(description of the need)* and we think *(initiative)* can be part of the solution. **Example:** New-hire associates need a way to ramp up to their new roles quickly and we think a better onboarding program can be part of the solution.
Part 2: Assume that your solution is the right one. Consider two or three "what if" scenarios and then think through assumptions or questions to be answered related to each "what if" scenario. **What-If Scenario Example:** *What if we designed a four-week immersive simulation? We could break it down by weeks and really make sure new associates know how to do our most-common project type by the end of four weeks.* **Assumptions or Questions** Based on your "what if" scenario, generate a list of possible assumptions and questions you have about the problem. • *What makes ramp-up hard for new hires?* • *How long has it taken our best associates to become productive?* • *How much time does it take for someone to become proficient at a single project type if that's all they are learning to do?* • *Have we considered other possible reasons for a slow ramp-up besides how we onboard people?* • *Who supports new hires now in learning their roles and the project work? Is there sufficient time available to teach new hires?* This technique blends problem refinement with ideation of possible solutions. It can be a useful tool when you don't get to do much pre-design meeting perspective gathering.

Get visual as part of ideating. Get people drawing rather than just talking. Draw ideas or create quick mock-ups to help people visualize a potential solution. Figure 7-6 is an example of some very basic screen mockups or storyboards to help people visualize the flow of an e-learning experience. None of this ended up getting used as shown, but it was hugely useful in helping the team—which was unfamiliar with e-learning—visualize how content could be presented in this format.

Figure 7-6. Quick Sketches of Possible E-Learning Interactions

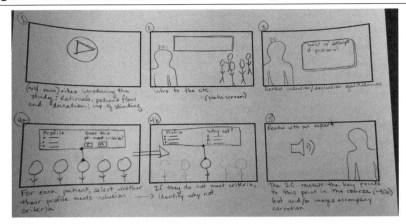

Obviously, such sketches do not require artistic talent!

Create Functional Prototypes

Now that you've got some great ideas, will they resonate? Will they really fit within your constraints? Find out by building and testing some functional prototypes that simulate the learner's experience. Many organizations use multi-day design meetings and include the stakeholders in a full day of prototyping. Others will do prototyping off-site and bring those prototypes back to the client for reaction. What matters most is that:

- you allocate time for it
- you involve your stakeholders in some fashion so they have buy-in
- you get quick reactions from target users and stakeholders to what you've prototyped.

Think of your initial prototypes as "sacrificial designs" that allow users to react and evaluate so you can refine them before you expend money and effort on development.

Functional prototypes should not be fancy; they should be quick to make and easy to throw away. You also don't need to prototype every idea you come up with.

The goal is for you to:

- Prototype key activities or tools that might be expensive to make so they can quickly be tested to verify feasibility. Does your solution fit into your constraints? Can you build your idea in the time you have? Within the budget you have? Within the technology or environmental constraints you have? With the skills you (or your team) have?
- Prototype where you need to verify the user experience: Is what you're designing easy to use, enjoyable to use, and valuable from the learner's point of view?
- Prototype what team members might struggle to have a common vision for: Does everyone understand what a solution will look like and include? A prototype is a fantastic way to get everyone on the same page in terms of understanding.

Figure 7-7 is an example of a rudimentary prototype of an activity we wanted to use to kick off a workshop. We had an idea for a quick game that could illustrate the environmental challenges field-based pharmaceutical sales reps faced when gaining access to a key decision maker. We were unsure the game would resonate. This prototype helped us very quickly get an answer (which was "yes").

Figure 7-7. Rudimentary Prototype

A prototype that we tested as part of a design meeting with a client.

Prototyping can occur on paper or be done digitally. We're big advocates of paper, but we know many people struggle to allow themselves to draw. There are prototyping tools (including PowerPoint) that enable you to create simple, clean screens without doing any actual programming. You insert hyperlinks to simulate user actions and allow the user to go through it. With that said, paper is often a better means of really thinking through the screens needed to deliver a specific user experience.

Here's your list of requirements to create a paper prototype:

- **Plenty of paper**—If your solution will be a digital one, use grid paper designed for the platform you're designing for. If you are mapping out a workshop activity, use flipchart paper.
- **Crayons, markers, or colored pencils**—Black and blue pencils work in a crunch, but colored pencils help you distinguish between various parts of the user interface if you are prototyping a digital solution.
- **Scissors and tape**—to hold things together and make it easy to move things around.
- **Sticky notes and index cards**—You can use them to make quick and dirty card decks for sorting activities, to cover and then reveal information, or any other number of things.
- **Representative content**—you will struggle to really test a prototype if it doesn't include any representative content. A common mistake is to include "Latin text" or placeholder text to represent scenarios,

  questions, or explanations. Things seem to work . . . until you attempt to build your solution with actual content that doesn't fit into the solution you mocked up and "tested." This representative content helps you test instructional value, your user interface design (does the volume of content required fit into the space you've crafted?), and your user experience. (Will the content be enjoyable to consume in this fashion? Will it be understandable? Will the activity be relevant to the learner?)

If opting for digital output instead of paper, you have lots of tool choices. You can use PowerPoint, but we recommend tools specifically designed for prototyping such as Marvel, Balsamiq, or for more sophisticated skillsets, Adobe XD. Marvel has a very cool tool called POP (which stands for "prototyping on paper") that allows you to photograph sketches you've made with your phone, and then upload them to POP. From there you can insert hyperlinks to simulate user actions. It's amazingly fast and easy. We've included an example in Figure 7-8. This was an early prototype of a game that eventually became TE Town (featured in the book *Play to Learn* that Sharon co-authored with Karl Kapp).

Figure 7-8. Digital Prototyping

The application POP enables you to sketch things on paper, take photos of your sketches, and create hotlinks to simulate user interactions. It's an extremely fast prototyping tool that lets you test and iterate quickly.

Iteration Checkpoint: Does the Prototype Work?

The beauty of quick prototypes is that you can get quick data. Have target learners test the early prototypes and watching as they interact with what you've made. Observe and ask:

- How engaging is this experience?
- How easy is it to understand what you need to do?
- How relevant does it seem to your work context and learning needs?

As the design team, also ask yourselves these things:

- Can we produce this solution within our constraints?
- How effective do we believe it will be in solving our problem and meeting our instructional goal and our learning objectives?

Work on Your Own

Invite a co-worker or two to help you brainstorm (ideate) a great onboarding reference tool for new hires.

After you brainstorm ideas, draw your solution out as a mobile or desktop app. Then either sketch your idea onto paper or download a prototyping tool (such as POP by Marvel, Balsamiq, or Adobe XD) and create a simple prototype of your idea that you can test with someone who is new to your company.

What do they tell you about how engaging it was? How easy it was to understand? How relevant it was for them as a new hire?

Then consider what it might take for you to build out your idea in terms of resources such as skill, money, and time.

Summary

Ideation and prototyping are powerful tools for designing solutions that resonate with actual learners—and not just stakeholders. Ensuring your initial design actually meets the needs of the organization and learners is the essence of our fourth principle, prototype before you refine. The next chapter gets you beyond prototyping into development of your solutions.

Refine and Develop

In This Chapter:
- Four techniques for refining and developing
- The power of UX testing
- How to pilot what you create
- The importance of iteration checkpoints

In both the traditional design thinking model and our LXD Framework, the step title is iterate, but the reality is that you must stop iterating at some point and develop, test, and refine. The biggest lesson we've learned when developing solutions is to avoid building the entire solution before asking for input. It is a recipe for massive editing and revision. Instead, we like to baby-step people to a finished solution. This chapter outlines tools and techniques that can help you move beyond initial prototype to finished solution.

Figure 8-1. The LXD Framework

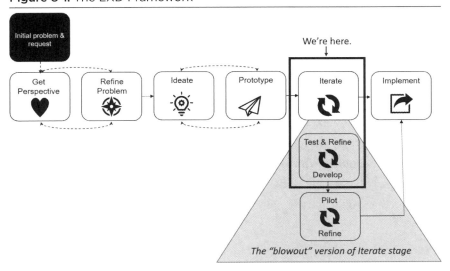

Design Proofs

A design proof is a means of proving that the design is valid. It serves three purposes:

- **It helps you verify that your design works as you transition into development.** You will create an initial version of each learning activity as part of this design proof. By doing so, you verify that the content you wanted to include will work in the activity. You also verify that the activity itself is a good one, with "good" defined as one where people learn from it and enjoy doing it. It differs from the prototype in that you've fully programmed it (if it is a digital solution) and you've incorporated select graphics and content into it.

- **It helps your stakeholders envision the solution more fully and verify the accuracy of the content you plan to include.** It helps ensure that everyone on the project team—stakeholders, subject matter experts, learners, and you—are on the same page regarding what the solution will look like and be like to use.

- **It helps clarify the content requirements of the solution.** Someone either must find or generate content for any solution you devise. The design proof helps crystalize the amount of effort that will be needed to either get or create this content.

Design proofs are one step past your initial prototypes while not being finished products, which means they can still flex a lot. As a rule of thumb, we assume that about 40 percent of the content or interactions we describe within a design proof may change. In fact, the design proof can help people identify what to keep and what to change. Don't ever refine a design proof to the point that it causes you pain to delete something you included in it.

For stakeholders who are not used to this kind of process, their knee-jerk reaction may be "It's not done!" or "It's broken!" For that reason, here are two best practices to facilitate a smooth review:

- **Selective review team.** The design proof should not necessarily be sent to the entire project team. Instead, share design proofs with just the core team who approved the design and now need to see the "proof" to confirm that it looks the way the design made it sound. For SMEs or executives, it may do more harm than good if they don't understand what they're looking at. Plus, it won't generate goodwill if they think they have to spend hours "editing" what was intended to be placeholders. You know your team; choose reviewers strategically.
- **Review prompts.** You can share design proofs with instructions that help focus the reviewer's attention on the right things. Each deliverable has aspects that require stakeholder approval before moving forward, and calling those out before they even open the link or document helps get them in the right mindset. For example, at design proof, we will often call out the 2 Fs: functionality and flow. We ask reviewers to:
  - Make sure all the activities work the way they expect.
  - Confirm all the necessary content is accounted for and is presented in a logical sequence.

If you review one of our design proofs, you'll also notice yellow notes sprinkled throughout, like, "Note to [client]: This is a placeholder graphic; we will replace with a modified version of the image on page 8 of the product brochure" or "Note to [client]: After reviewing the content, we recommend three review questions instead of five." These prompts and notes help to curate the experience: to clarify what they're seeing and explain anything that's different from the design.

Figures 8-2 and 8-3 contain a few screens of a design proof for an e-learning module. You can see that the goal here is not to fully build out the solution, it's to help verify the design. If you are crafting a workshop-style solution, you may opt for a detailed outline and description of each activity as your design proof. We've included an excerpt from a detailed workshop design in Figure 8-4 as an example.

Figure 8-2. Design Proof #1

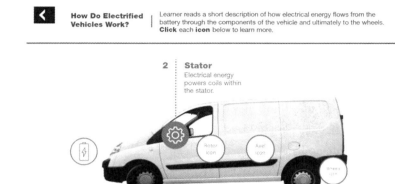

This design proof shows an activity developed with only select graphics and content.

Figure 8-3. Design Proof #2

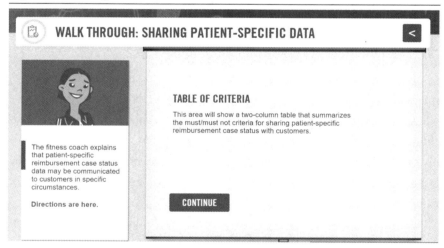

This design proof shows a screen developed with content descriptions rather than full scripting.

Figure 8-4. Design Proof #3

Session 3: Build Your EQ

Description: This two-hour session helps participants recognize the impact that high or low EQ has on the workplace environment and their own success. It also emphasizes the correlation between high EQ and the perceptions others have of their leadership efficacy (66 percent of effective leadership). Participants will explore tactics for reframing negative situations and optimizing their EQ.

Program objectives this session helps support or enables participants to achieve:
- Evaluate their own emotional intelligence; use this evaluation to craft a plan for maximizing it so they can most effectively work with others to achieve business outcomes.

Pre-Session Work	Post-Session Work
• EQ 2.0 pp. 1-57 and EQ assessment • No Ceiling, No Walls pp. 117-144 • Schedule a one-on-one meetup within the designated timeframe	• Feedback gathering exercise • No Ceiling, No Walls pp. 45-115 • Schedule a one-on-one meetup within the designated timeframe

Time Required: 2 hours

Activities and Content
Opening Check-In for Participants: • Right now, I feel . . . • My goal related to EQ is . . . • My intention for this session is . . . **Time Required:** 10 minutes
Activity: Emotional Survey: Participants identify negative and positive emotions they have experienced at work in the past 48 hours. They rate the intensity of the emotions and the factors that contributed to the emotion. They then think of a coworker and identify emotions they witnessed in that individual, their perception of the intensity of the emotion, and the affect it had on them. They then compare their descriptors against the emotions chart to categorize those emotions (happy, sad, angry, afraid, ashamed).
Lecturette: Facilitator explains the four quadrants that make up EQ (self-awareness, self-management, social awareness, relationship management—what highs and lows look like in each quadrant, the impact it has on others, and how the highs and lows correlate to operating above or below the line (reference to Session 1). **Time Required:** 20 minutes

This is an example of detailed design for a workshop program module. The detailed design allows stakeholders and learners to evaluate before you invest time in creating full set of materials.

UX Testing

User experience testing, or UX testing, helps ensure that people understand what they are supposed to do while using your solution. With digital solutions, it involves observing learners attempting to complete various tasks and seeing how easily they can do so without help from you and without confusion on their part. With classroom solutions, you want to do UX and playtesting on all games or activities so you can verify your directions are clear and the activity is understandable and meets your objectives.

For example, in a digital solution, user testing helps you verify:

- Learners can successfully navigate to information easily.
- Learners understand directions to games and activities that are embedded into the app.
- Learners can perform essential tasks such as logging into the app, updating settings, or using a search function.
- Learners can read the text on screens and accurately interpret icons such as "next," "menu," or "go back."

You can repeat the UX testing process for each new feature or activity. Ideally every unique component or activity in a digital solution should go through UX testing. As a general guideline, test anything that will be new to a user group. The goal is to assess:

- Is this easy for you to use? (If it is a digital solution, navigational features are easy to locate and use. Processes are easy to execute and don't require excessive numbers of steps. If it is a solution that is embedded somewhere, the user can easily find it within a larger system. If it is a live solution, then users understand how to get started and how to execute directions.)
- Is this easy to understand what to do? (Your next action or your options are obvious and clear to you.)
- Is this a solution you find enjoyable to use? (You are engaged by what you see, hear, or get to do.)
- Does this solution help you learn X (with X equaling whatever objectives the activity is designed to teach).

To help keep usability testing on track, you can create test scripts to outline the tasks you want a user to complete while you observe or to get feedback on remotely if they are not where you can observe them. Ask them to think out loud while they execute the test steps and take notes on what you hear as well as on what you observe them doing.

Table 8-1 shows a sample test script for a digital app with notes from the tester. A simple script like this can easily be adapted for non-digital solutions as well. The goal is to identify what learners need to do and then observe how easily they can execute on each "what." In general, test scripts should avoid including the "how" of doing something. You are testing the usability of the solution, which includes the ease with which users figure out the "how" associated with each task they need to do.

Table 8-1. Test Script for a Digital Learning Solution

Test Step	Observer Notes and Learner "Think Out Loud" Comments
1) Log into the solution.	*Learner struggled to create a good password. Kept having to revisit guidelines.* *Liked the easy-to-read fonts and prompts in entry fields.*
2) Locate module 1.	*Learner didn't immediately recognize that "hamburger icon" was where menu could be accessed. Once she located it, she easily found module 1.*
3) Complete the activities in module 1.	*Learner easily understood sorting activity but was confused by "product picker" activity and struggled to manipulate the scrolling tool that enabled selection of a specific product.*

Get Real: The Power of UX Testing

A few years ago we were building a large-scale mobile game that was actually numerous mini-games within a gamified environment. Learners could construct a town, region by region, and build selling mastery by playing a series of mini-games.

We used an independent third-party solution to help us do UX testing of early versions of the mini-games. This tool allowed us to record users playing our game while "thinking out loud." We gave users a set of three actions to perform after logging into the game:

1. Start constructing your first region of the town.
2. Play one mini-game.
3. Locate your standings in the game after playing.

We were dismayed by how confused they were by our user interface. They bypassed all the directions at the front of the game that explained how they were to select their first region and start construction. They bypassed the demo of how to play the mini-game. Our icon for locating standings was not intuitive to them either.

The good news in all of this was that we tested early. We hadn't built a lot so redoing it was relatively painless and inexpensive. We learned a tremendous amount with a simple 15-minute usability test that paid huge dividends for our development team later.

Sprints

A "sprint" is a concept borrowed from Agile software development. In Agile software development, a product is produced via a series of sprints that last from one to four weeks. A sprint-based format gives flexibility and allows you to iterate based on testing results. The goal is for the development team to produce a "minimum viable product," or MVP, at the conclusion of each one. The team is aligned on exactly what "done" looks like for the short time period. In the NxStage solution we built (see chapter 14), the sprints looked a little bit like what we've outlined in Table 8-2.

The team plans exactly which components or features will be built during the sprint time period (one to four weeks) and assigns the work to team members. At the conclusion of each sprint, you perform the UX testing described in the preceding section. After you finish the UX test, you and your client jointly agree on what revisions to make. The execution of the revisions is part of the next sprint, along with any new development work that needs to happen.

Table 8-2. Example of a Sprint-Based Development Plan for a Web App

Sprint	Duration	Software Version	What User Will Be Able to Do
1	2 weeks	0.1	Log in to the app; view the main screen.
2	2 weeks	0.2	Select the "Learn" option from main screen, view list of modules, and complete one module in full.
3	3 weeks	0.3	Locate and complete all modules available within learn (a total of 7).
4	4 weeks	0.4	Select the "troubleshooting" option from main screen and access 5 frequent troubleshooting codes and steps for fixing each one.
5	2 weeks	0.5	Use the search feature to search by key words or topics.
6	2 weeks	1.0—first official release to broad pool of learners	Connect to the online social community and exchange messages.

The UX testing that occurs at the conclusion of each sprint will result in the team identifying potential refinements. These get categorized into two buckets:

- **Must-have refinements:** Items that belong here represent errors that must be fixed, significant usability problems, or critical missing information.
- **Nice-to-have refinements:** These items are things that might enhance the experience but are not critical to a positive experience. These can be put onto a "backlog" list, which means you want to keep them for consideration for later updates you might make after your initial version 1.0 release (if you get additional budget).

If you aren't building a software solution, you can still work in sprints and do UX testing at the conclusion of each one.

Regardless of what you might be developing, you can still follow the three general rules for running sprint-based development:

- Keep sprint durations between one and four weeks with two to three-week sprints being optimal lengths.
- Test and identify refinements at the conclusion of each sprint cycle with people who represent your target user group.
- Categorize refinements identified into the "must-have" or "nice-to-have" buckets. Adjust future sprint plans based on the refinements you must incorporate into your next version of the solution.

In an e-learning project where you use Storyline or Rise to create a course, you can create sprint cycles around draft versions of the course (Table 8-3). As you go through the cycles, the refinements required should decrease. You still follow the general rules we just outlined.

Table 8-3. Example of a Sprint-Based Development Plan for a Storyline E-Learning Course

Sprint	Duration	Materials version	Target	% Change Anticipated
1	2 weeks	0.1	Design proof of course	40%
2	1 week	0.2	Fully functional module 1 + testing and review	30%
3	3 weeks	0.3	Full alpha of course + review	25%
4	2 weeks	0.4	Full beta of course + review	15%
5	2 weeks	1.0	Final course (a.k.a. "gold master")	0%
6	2 weeks	1.0—first official release to broad pool of learners	Connect to the online social community and exchange messages.	

Pilot Sessions and Beta Versions

Perfection should not be the enemy of "good enough," but it often can be. Stakeholders can get mired in delivering a perfect solution, particularly if they have outsourced development. Lots of time and dollars get wasted as teams burn hours making small revisions. Ideally, you will push out a version of your solution that is good enough for pilot or beta testing on a larger group of users. This group of users can be a blend of stakeholders and target users, but the feedback from your target users should be viewed as most meaningful and important. If they don't understand something or don't find it useful or relevant, the stakeholders need to listen and respect the value of the feedback.

A good pilot or beta test includes these things:

- Opportunity for learners to fully experience your solution as you intend it to be used by the broader population and under the same conditions you expect it to be used.
- Ample time for getting feedback from pilot users and observing them using your solution.
- A skilled facilitator who manages group feedback well, not allowing one person to dominate the discussion and carefully ensuring that all perspectives get heard. Quieter voices often disagree with a loud one but choose not to speak up.

If your solution is a software solution, then beta is going to mean a version of the software that gets released for users to experience. In such cases, you may or may not be observing their usage. Your job will be to solicit feedback and have some mechanism for people to report issues they may experience. You can consider including a link to an online survey within your web app. If your beta user pool is relatively small and you can capture emails, you can also consider emailing a survey to users or requesting participation in an online feedback session. A small group of users can provide helpful feedback. What you won't get is feedback from anyone who chose not to use your app. You will want to consider some way to follow up with all beta testers to find out if any of them chose not to participate after volunteering to beta test.

If your solution is a live event or workshop of some sort, then "beta" is likely to mean your pilot. In this instance you pull together a representative group of learners and execute the live event. You may be the facilitator of this event or observing the individual who is. If the event is a daylong experience, you may opt to have a couple of timepoints throughout the day where you seek feedback from participants on the activities in terms of their value, clarity, and interest. If it is a shorter event (one hour to a half day), you may simply collect feedback at the conclusion of the event.

If you are truly delivering a multifaceted learning experience that spans the full learning journey from "Notice" to "Maintain Use Over Time," you need to get comprehensive feedback on each facet of the journey. Appendix 9 is a sample pilot evaluation tool we created based on Will Thalheimer's 2018 book *Performance-Focused Smile Sheets*.

With either a digital solution or a live event, you once again must decide between must-have changes and nice-to-have changes.

Must-have changes should be any change that fixes a clear problem that hinders usability or accuracy of your solution. Nice-to-have changes are often text edits or aesthetic changes that will not affect usability or learning effectiveness. This decision point takes you to your final tool.

Iteration Checkpoints

In earlier chapters, we outlined a variety of tools that help you find that "sweet spot" that reflects human-centered design. You don't want to waste all that effort you expended gathering perspective in the early stages of your work. So, as you go through each develop and refine sprint or stage, revisit your persona and your strategy blueprint and verify you are staying true to it:

- Will the experience you are building meet the needs of your personas? Have you unintentionally deviated in some way? If so, how should you refine things to get you back on track?
- Is the solution going to solve the challenges and achieve the aspirations you defined in your strategy blueprint? If it's off-target, how do you get realigned?
- As you develop, are you uncovering any new constraints (such as technology challenges) that you must address?

The goal of an iteration checkpoint is to ensure that you don't lose sight of the humans (learners) who should be the focal point of your efforts.

Work on Your Own

Reflect on a project you've recently completed. Consider how you might have organized that project into smaller "sprints" that would have enabled you to get frequent feedback on it while it was under construction.

If you focus primarily on live events, review the pilot evaluation tool in appendix 9. Notice how the items all relate to how applicable the content and activities are to the individual's work. How might this type of questioning influence the feedback you get on the solutions you develop?

Summary

Eventually you must stop designing and start building if you want a finished solution. However, that doesn't mean you shouldn't continue to seek perspective to stay aligned to the sweet spot. The tools and techniques outlined in this chapter are mechanisms to help you move into and through development while staying true to the people you are building your solution for.

As you finish designing and developing your solution, it's time to implement it, which is the subject of the next chapter and the start of section 4.

SECTION 4
IMPLEMENT AND EVALUATE

Implement

In This Chapter:
- The components of an implementation plan
- What measures you should monitor
- The risks to mitigate

Think of implementation as your final step in "strategy activation." Previous chapters explained how to define your problem, get perspective, ideate, prototype, and develop a solution. This chapter outlines the components of a good plan to help you implement the solution you devised.

Figure 9-1. The LXD Framework

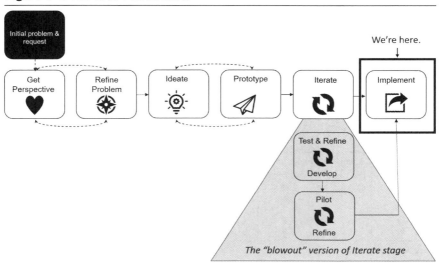

What's in an Implementation Plan?

The entire learning journey you devised describes how you will solve a problem. So, by being thoughtful along the way, you have already woven in many aspects of implementation planning into your entire learning journey by considering and ideating on the activities a learner will experience as part of each step. As a quick refresher, Figure 9-2 shows a summary of the learning journey map with the steps defined and the desired outcomes of each step. These are the steps you need to support with your implementation plan:

- Get people to notice a need to learn or change.
- Get people to commit to learning.
- Provide a means for them to learn and practice the new information or skill.
- Incorporate follow-up repetition and elaboration on what they learned (transfer this into the workplace).
- Reflect and explore further.
- Sustain performance over time.

Figure 9-2. Blank Learning Journey Map

Phase	Prepare		Acquire Knowledge & Skill	Build Memory & Try Using on the Job		Maintain over Time
Step	1. Notice	2. Commit	3. Learn and Practice	4. Repeat and Elaborate	5. Reflect and Explore	6. Sustain usage
Desired Outcomes	Accept the need to learn	Make time to learn	Engage, find relevance	Remain committed, gain confidence	Go deeper, learn more, share early successes	Consistently use new skill or knowledge, achieve buisness results
Key actions or activities						
Thoughts & Feelings						
Magical Moments						
Miserable Moments						

In addition to your learning journey, the strategy blueprint we explained in chapter 4 is a useful tool as you define an implementation plan. Together, these tools can help you formulate an implementation plan that outlines the logistics of delivering the experience you've mapped out for learners. This plan summarizes:

- what needs to happen
- how it will happen
- when it needs to happen
- who needs to be involved
- who is accountable for any given step and for the overall endeavor (this one is key)
- measures you will monitor and how you will report progress
- risks and their likelihood, with high-risk issues having a mitigation plan associated with them.

Depending on the size of your endeavor, your plan may be a simple one-page document or a document that is several pages long that gets organized as an administrator's guide. Both large and small-scale plans need to be thought out, revisited frequently, and iterated on as needed. If an initiative is worth spending weeks and months designing and implementing, it is worth spending time planning out the logistics, the accountability, and how you'll monitor progress. Table 9-1 identifies things for you to consider within each bullet we listed above. If it sounds a bit like a project plan, it is because it is: Implementation is an activity. You can't just build something and hope everyone shows up. It takes work to roll out an initiative and maintain it after it gets rolled out. Remember, failure to plan is the fastest path to failure to achieve results.

Table 9-1. Implementation Plan Components

Component	Best Practices	Things to Think About
What, how, and who Describe what activities will occur, how they will occur, and who is the recipient of the action	Keep things visually simple; avoid a complex, color-coded diagram that requires someone to serve as an interpreter. Include information that identifies your "how" of a rollout: will it be in waves, by function, start small and go bigger, and so on. Specify the "who." Clarify the make-up of each group, who will trigger the activity, and who will participate in the activity. Include plan monitoring as an activity and specify who does it; if snafus arise after you've rolled things out to your first group, for example, who is attending to the rollout and adjusting the plan?	• Don't forget to include the "invisible" activities required to enable the more visible ones. Do you need to recruit facilitators or mentors? Do you need to coordinate messaging with the communications team? • Are you being realistic with the activities? Can you really execute everything you list?
Timeline and target dates Determine when each activity will occur, and what timing is critical.	If you are doing a time-based initiative that starts on a specific calendar date, be sure to work backward from that date to ensure you allow adequate time for any pre-launch activities. If you are spacing activities out over time, account for that spacing in your planning. Also account for holidays.	• Are you allowing enough time? • Are resources available in the timing you specify?

Component	Best Practices	Things to Think About
Accountability Identify the role accountable as well as any roles that have major involvement.	Identify the role accountable for executing the action rather than specifying people by name. (For example, "CEO" is better than "Susan Smith." You want to know who has functional accountability for an action; if you are implementing a program that will be a long-standing one, you also want one that will endure past any specific employee.) Avoid assigning multiple people and roles accountability. When everyone is accountable, no one is. Note: The stakeholder map from chapter 4 can be helpful here.	• How will you hold people accountable? • What's the consequence if someone does not do what they are supposed to do?
Assumptions Specify the people, materials, physical space, budget, or media required to execute a particular activity or event that's part of implementation.	Don't assume people will all understand what's required to make things happen. Spell out assumptions about any reproduction required, involved from other functional areas, items to purchase, and so on. Make sure you can get the resources you need: Verify how you will get printing done, media produced, or funding secured to pay for production costs.	• Have you "checked your thinking" on your assumptions? Who has validated them? • Are you being realistic or optimistic?

Table 9-1. Implementation Plan Components (cont.)

Component	Best Practices	Things to Think About
Measurement gathering Include identified measures within the plan.	Identify specific timepoints for gathering measurements. Identify personnel who will do the measurement collection and analysis.	• Can you get the measures you need? If not you, then who? • What is the appropriate time point for taking measurements? • How will measures be reported and to whom will they be reported?
Risks Every plan has risks; figure out yours and identify ways to mitigate any you label as "high."	You cannot mitigate every risk so focus on those you perceive as high. Categorize risks as high, medium, or low based on how likely they are to occur and how significant its impact to your initiative would be if it did. A risk that would be catastrophic and has at least a 30% chance of happening should be considered "high." A risk that's fairly likely to happen but would have minimal impact can be labeled "medium" or "low."	• Again, are you being realistic or optimistic as you identify and rate risks?

The Get Real sidebar contains details about our own implementation plan for rolling out design thinking practices. It shows how we used the strategy blueprint tool (featured in chapter 4) to inform our implementation plan (Figure 9-3). Table 9-2 features an excerpt of our plan showing milestone dates, tasks to achieve, and people responsible.

Get Real: Rolling Out Design Thinking at Bottom-Line Performance

When rolling out design thinking tools and techniques internally at Bottom-Line Performance, we did not have bandwidth to create an extensive plan. However, we did craft a strategy blueprint and a simple logistical plan that included most of the elements listed earlier. (We did not identify risks formally, though we did discuss them.) Here's what our strategy blueprint looked like (Figure 9-3).

Figure 9-3. Strategy Blueprint to Roll Out Design Thinking

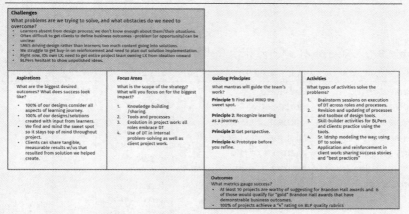

We created our strategy in February 2019. We wanted implementation completed by December 2019, to realize quantifiable impact by no later than April 2020. Using the strategy blueprint as a guide, we formulated a simple logistical plan. We then assembled a simple implementation plan. By doing so, we proactively spotted potential problems before we encountered them. A few of the problems we caught and adjusted before rollout. An obvious theme of over-optimism emerged, specifically:

- over-optimism about our own bandwidth
- over-optimism about other people's bandwidth
- over-optimism on when we could start; when we plotted things out, we could see we needed more prep time to get materials in place and to prep for sessions we planned to do.

This level of over-optimism is not unique to us; it's a common challenge when organizations prepare to implement anything. A plan helps curb and control that over-optimism if the stakeholders challenge each other on the realism of the plan. An excerpt of our plan is shown in Table 9-1. It focuses on activities one, two, and five listed in our strategy blueprint.

In addition to this logistical plan, we identified our leadership meetings as the place we would be held accountable for implementation. Sharon reported to the executive team; Laura to the functional level team. Each of us had a goal related to implementation and reported on progress as part of the weekly meetings we had with our teams.

Table 9-2. Excerpt of a Logistical Rollout Plan

Activity	Mar–Apr 2019	May–Aug 2019	Sep–Dec 2019
Brainstorm sessions with Agile teams on execution of design thinking across roles and processes.	Facilitate perspective-gathering sessions that include every member of the 5 project teams. (Laura, Sharon) Session 1 (Challenges, aspirations, experience maps): • Teams 1 and 2 (March 4) • Teams 3 and 4 (March 13) • Team 5 (March 26) Session 2: (Learning Journeys): • Teams 1 and 2 (April 1) • Teams 3 and 4 (April 15) • Team 5 (April 18)	• Facilitate discussions on key tactics for "finding and minding" the sweet spot with the 4 functional teams during weekly team meetings. • May: Instructional Design Team (Laura) • June: Multimedia Team (Sharon) • July: Project Mgmt. Team (Sharon) • August: Learning Technologist Team (Laura)	N/A

Activity	Mar–Apr 2019	May–Aug 2019	Sep–Dec 2019
Revise and update processes and toolbox.	Design thinking tools added as a "Quick Reference" sub-menu item on the company intranet. Links take user to descriptions of tools and how to use them. (Laura)	May: Design thinking activities and best practices are included appropriately in procedure documentation. (Laura) July: Design thinking principles and processes are incorporated into each function's quality rubric so projects can be evaluated against them. (Laura)	N/A
Apply and reinforce in project work; share success stories	Use weekly "Breaking News" forum and the company intranet to highlight success stories internally. (Sharon)		September: Share case studies at eXLearn conference (annual company conference) (Sharon, Laura plus others as defined)

This is a simple plan, but it identifies what needs to happen, when it needs to happen, and how it will get done. The "who" is also specified as appropriate (which teams are doing what, and when). The plan also specifies who is accountable for doing each task. For a more robust implementation template that incorporates the best practice components we describe in this chapter, see appendix 10.

Measures to Monitor

When you select measures to include in a strategy blueprint, consider how easily you can monitor progress against them. These are the measures you want to track as you move into implementation of your solution. In our design thinking rollout, measurement and monitoring was specified at the company and functional level; Sharon (company level) and Laura (functional level) had quarterly goals related to the plan that we reported on at our respective weekly meetings. The strategy blueprint specified two measures:

- 10 "award-worthy" projects by April, with six of them that we would feel capable of achieving a "Gold" level Brandon Hall award.
- A 4 rating (out of 5) on every project we delivered per the guidelines of our internal quality rubrics. (A 4 rating equated to a solution showing excellent implementation, comparable to other strong examples.)

These measures were relatively simple to track over time. We reviewed projects quarterly, which meant we'd have relatively frequent data. Brandon Hall awards have two award windows annually so that was another fairly frequent measure. We likely would have benefited from an additional measure that had a monthly frequency for the first several months' time. Bottom line: Keep your measures simple and make sure they are trackable. Assign a single person to be accountable for tracking as much as possible and specify frequency of reporting.

Risks to Mitigate

Ideally, you will document risks and define mitigation strategies as part of your implementation plan. The major risk we discussed was the upswing in project loads that would make it difficult for us to plan and for people to attend or focus on specific skill-builders we hoped to create. While not referenced in the excerpt shown in Table 9-1, our full plan included skill-builder sessions we hoped to facilitate throughout the summer months.

This risk indeed became reality, and the sessions we planned for June and July never occurred. However, everything else we planned did get executed. When we arrived at September (the end of our planned implementation) we saw that our efforts from March through August had paid off. Without prompting, every single session presented at our annual company conference included references to:

- finding and minding the sweet spot
- empathy mapping and experience mapping
- learning journeys.

Two case study sessions at the conference featured complete success stories of use of design thinking techniques. The theme of design thinking and crafting exceptional learning experiences underpinned everyone's messages and examples. This was not an outcome articulated in the original blueprint, but it was a notable, qualitative result of our efforts.

Our lesson learned was to plan for risks but also recognize that iteration and flexibility need to be part of the plan. You can still achieve results even if you don't achieve perfection. What matters most is having a plan that you can adjust as needed. No plan at all—and no focus on aspirations or metrics—would have led to failure.

Work on Your Own

Think about an initiative you've rolled out, or perhaps consider the Honest Conversations initiative we describe in chapter 2. Consider what you did well in implementing that initiative and what you did poorly. Analyze:

- The elements of the learning journey you put into your plan and any you omitted. Did you, for example, focus all your implementation planning on step 3 of the journey, learn and practice, or did your implementation plan support all the steps of the journey?
- What elements of your plan matched the ones we recommend including in this chapter? (See Table 9-2. Does your plan include elements that ours did not? How did those add value to you?)

Summary

Good implementation planning matters, but don't let perfect be the enemy of a "good enough" plan. Make sure accountability is clear and support exists throughout the organization for your initiative. Without senior-level support, most initiatives die. Plan for the journey: The learning events you facilitate are less important than the things you do to help people notice the need to learn, help them commit, reinforce and elaborate, and allow for reflection and exploration to deepen skill and knowledge. Finally, metrics matter. If you don't have a target to hit, then you won't hit it. The next chapter gets into how to evaluate your training and development program within the design thinking process.

# Evaluate

In This Chapter:
- The reasons to evaluate
- How evaluation fits into the design thinking process
- The different evaluation models

At its core, design thinking is a problem-solving process. This means that at some point you will want to verify that you solved the problem. Evaluation is how you verify that what you created worked.

Many clients we talk to are not evaluating training initiatives at all, a fact supported by ATD's research report, *Evaluating Learning: Getting to Measurements That Matter* (ATD 2016). They found that only 35 percent out of 199 talent development professionals surveyed reported their organizations evaluated the business results of learning programs to any extent.

In this chapter we hope to persuade you to do some level of evaluation to answer the question, "Is the problem solved?" Entire books are written on the topic of program evaluation, so this chapter isn't intended as a step-by-step guide. Instead, we provide an overview of why evaluation is critical and identify possible models for you to consider.

Why Evaluate?

By not evaluating your programs, you cheat yourself out of true completion of the project and seeing the business results of your efforts. After you've defined a problem, gathered the perspectives of the stakeholders and learners, designed the learning journey, prototyped, developed, and user-tested the solution, not knowing how the learners fared using your solution devalues the steps you took early in the process. In other words, why worry about creating a usable, effective learning experience if you don't verify that the solution was usable and effective post-deployment?

There are three main reasons that make evaluation a worthwhile pursuit:

- **Confirm efficacy.** If you did a good job verifying the business problem, you should have solid business metrics identified to help quantify success or failure. If that's the case, you should be able to assess:
    - whether the learning objectives were met
    - whether transfer happened and job performance was positively changed
    - the degree that performance change affected the organization.
- **Identify opportunities for improvement.** Much like shying away from user testing, one reason people shy away from evaluation is because they're afraid of the results. "What if I find out the training solution was ineffective?" . . . well, what if? Let's play out the worst-case scenario: You execute an evaluation plan a year after launch. The results show that learners struggle to use the solution (or didn't even open it). No behavior change was realized, and no business results were achieved. Do you want an ineffective solution sitting on the web server for eternity? Or would you rather take a fully developed solution that's not meeting expectations, make adjustments, and re-deploy a new and improved solution? Obviously, it's better for the organization if you modify and re-deploy than do nothing. An ineffective solution does not necessarily mean that your process was ineffective, as you'll see in Get Real: Things Change.
- **Show me the money.** The truth is, sometimes people within organizations develop training for training's sake. But more and more frequently senior leaders within organizations are holding people accountable for results. Senior leaders may not seek a full-blown return-on-investment (ROI) analysis, but they expect some kind of metric they can use to show positive outcomes for the business. For those that are practicing responsible instructional design, this should be great news! With a record of proven results, it's easier to justify access to learners, earlier inclusion into projects, and the budget you need to maintain your record of success.

Get Real: Things Change

Several years ago, we redesigned the onboarding process for animal caregivers at a life sciences company. The target learners worked in a sterile environment, which required unique materials that the mentors were eager to implement. However, less than five years after the materials were launched, we learned that those materials were never implemented effectively. What happened?

There were many reasons the materials had fallen out of favor with the onboarding mentors. One of the culprits was a language gap. An increase in employees who did not speak fluent English meant that mentors were having to improvise as best they could to meet the learners where they were. Another setback was changes to a highly-regulated environment; while the majority of the content was stable and accurate, having some outdated information diminished overall confidence in the materials. Onboarding mentors were doing what they thought was best, which often meant abandoning the training plan and materials.

These types of workplace changes are very familiar: they could be big changes (a process is relocated overseas, a new legislation changes how employees can communicate, a paper-and-pencil process is transitioned onto tablets) or small changes (a process owner goes on maternity leave during roll-out, or a hiring freeze is implemented). The point is, they can happen quickly and quietly; without intentional evaluation, these changes can silently derail a training initiative.

Evaluation Starts Early

Evaluation begins early in the project. In fact, once you have a clearly defined business problem, you've got the first component you need for your evaluation plan. Ideally, creating evaluation metrics even before the learning objectives will help preempt any ideas for solutions that sound good but won't truly get the job done. (The strategy blueprint featured in chapter 4 is a great place to document your project's success criteria and metrics.) As you begin brainstorming metrics, you may realize that it is difficult to isolate the effects of a training solution from other factors solely by looking at employee engagement or revenue numbers. Using a variety of metrics (and knowing what that metric is really measuring) can help mitigate that challenge.

Here's a fictionalized example based on a real project: You're leading a project to support a sales initiative with a goal of increasing annual revenue by 5 percent. That 5 percent revenue increase is your ultimate business goal—a top-line impact on the business that proves success or failure of the initiative. Now you can work backward to identify metrics that will show evidence of behavior change, retention, and understanding. These become project milestones after deployment, built-in "moments of truth" at which point you can either decide to proceed with the training as-is, or pivot to course-correct and optimize results. Plotted on a timeline, those metrics might look something like Table 10-1.

Table 10-1. Sample Evaluation Plan

	Deployment	3 Months	6 Months	12 Months
What Is Being Measured	Knowledge and retention	Transfer	Transfer and effects of transfer	Effects of transfer
Tactic	• Quick quiz 1 week post-workshop • Email campaign with multiple choice scenario sent each week	• Sales managers do a behavioral assessment during a regularly scheduled ride-along	• Sales managers do a behavioral assessment during ride-along • Program manager reviews CRM report	• End-of-year fiscal report
Metric	• Quiz score of 90% • 90% of scenario responses are correct	• 75% of sales reps are demonstrating new behaviors on the job	• 100% of sales reps are demonstrating new behaviors on the job • Customer inquiries have increased by 10%	• Revenue has increased by 5%

Now imagine you're six months post-deployment. Learners aced the post-workshop quiz and have enjoyed competing with other sales regions to answer the scenarios in the email campaign. But now, the sales managers are reporting back that they're seeing the behaviors carried out by less than 50 percent of their reps. The sales managers you've spoken with said sales reps are actively resistant to the new tactics, which you did not anticipate. Without these evaluation milestones built in, you could wait six more months until the revenue report is published to confirm that the initiative missed the mark. Or, you could get out there and talk to some sales reps to uncover the disconnect between what they know they are supposed to do, and what they are actually doing. This is a perfect demonstration of the iterative nature of design thinking: things change, and when they do, the learner is right back at the table with you to discover the best way forward.

Evaluation Models for Any Project

In this section we provide an overview of four evaluation models: the Kirkpatrick Four Levels of Evaluation, Will Thalheimer's Learning-Transfer Evaluation Model, the Phillips ROI Methodology, and the Brinkerhoff Success Case Method. If you find one that suits your project and want more information, all the models below have detailed resources cited.

The Kirkpatrick Four Levels of Evaluation

The Kirkpatrick Four Levels of Evaluation model is a widely accepted industry standard (Kirkpatrick and Kirkpatrick 2016). It describes evaluation of learning solution in four levels:

- **Level 1: Reaction.** Learner's reaction to the learning solution.
- **Level 2: Learning.** The knowledge, skills, attitude, confidence, and commitment gained as a result of the learning solution.
- **Level 3: Behavior.** Learning transfer to the job: on-the-job behavior changed as a result of the learning solution.
- **Level 4: Results.** Measurable outcomes the organization realized as a result of the learning solution.

Very few organizations measure learning transfer and organizational outcomes. When they measure only learner reaction and knowledge, it underscores the fact that many organizations are spending time and money designing learning events that are not focused on post-event results. By using design thinking to map a complete learning journey, it is easier to identify evaluation metrics that target Levels 3 and 4. In the example above, if sales manager ride-alongs are planned as an activity in the learning journey, then behavioral metrics from those ride-alongs are an obvious evaluative data point to plan for.

Learning-Transfer Evaluation Model

Will Thalheimer's Learning-Transfer Evaluation Model, or LTEM, highlights some of the nuance that you might not notice with the Kirkpatrick model (Thalheimer 2018). It directs the evaluation toward effective learning transfer, and accurately addresses learner perception as being of low to no value for assessing successful transfer. It is organized into eight tiers, starting with the highest value measures at the top and the most basic (and least reliable) measures of transfer at the bottom (Table 10-2). (You can see the full model in appendix 11.)

Table 10-2. The Eight Tiers of the Learning-Transfer Evaluation Model

Tier	Description
8	Effects of Transfer
7	Transfer
6	Task Competence
5	Decision-Making Competence
4	Knowledge
3	Learner Perceptions
2	Activity
1	Attendance

Because LTEM breaks measures down with more granular criteria and explanations, it helps to better inform what your data is actually measuring. For example, imagine you test learners' decision-making competence during a workshop. In this tier—tier 5—the model points out the difference between evaluating during the event versus several days or weeks later, as learners may forget these competencies without any reinforcement. It further specifies the difference between decision-making competence and task competence, which it defines as including both decision making and action taking. This distinction is not highlighted in other models and helps to point out exactly where on the evaluation spectrum your test falls.

Get Real: LTEM at Work

We recently used the LTEM model to evaluate a leadership program for women. The first evaluative method was a survey built using Thalheimer's "Performance-Focused Survey Questions," which he publishes and updates every year on his website, worklearning.com. The survey questions were designed to measure learner perception and knowledge (tiers 3-4). The second method was a collection of business metrics taken after the six-month program concluded. The client was delighted to discover that 23 percent of participants had received a promotion within eight months of completing the first session. Using LTEM, this correlates to "effects of transfer" (tier 8) and aligned with a primary goal of the program to increase the number of women eligible for higher-grade roles in the organization.

The Phillips ROI Methodology

The Phillips ROI Methodology takes a five-level approach to evaluation, which culminates in turning results into a financial component. Their five-level framework looks like this:

- **Level 1: Reaction and Planned Action.** Learner reaction to the learning solution and their planned actions.
- **Level 2: Learning.** The knowledge and skills gained as a result of the learning solution.
- **Level 3: Application and Implementation.** How learners are able to transfer the knowledge and skills to the job.
- **Level 4: Impact.** Whether the application of knowledge and skills resulted in measurable outcomes for the organization.
- **Level 5: ROI.** The return on investment (ROI) produced by the learning solution.

ROI is an often-discussed but rarely executed business equation:

$$\text{ROI (\%)} = \frac{\text{project benefits} - \text{project costs}}{\text{project costs}} \times 100$$

We've noticed that within the training and performance development industry, "ROI" has begun to be used as slang for any value-based data gathered on a project. To provide more guidance and consistency to ROI evaluation, the Phillips model is accompanied by a 12-step methodology designed specifically to help training programs evaluate true return on investment (Phillips and Phillips 2019).

Interestingly, according to the ROI Institute, only about 5 percent of programs should be evaluated at this level, reserving this type of in-depth data collection for the strategic, expensive projects with the most at stake.

Success Case Method

Robert Brinkerhoff's Success Case Method, described in his book *The Success Case Method: Find Out Quickly What's Working and What's Not*, involves identifying and evaluating the most and least successful results of a solution in the form of a case study of that result (Brinkerhoff 2003). Once these successful (or not) cases have been identified, it allows for a more qualitative approach for answering four questions:

- What is really happening?
- What results, if any, is the program helping to produce?
- What is the value of the results?
- How could the initiative be improved?

The qualitative approach is appealing for projects whose results can be difficult to quantify, such as soft skills and leadership training. The fact that this method provides yet another touchpoint to circle back with learners makes it very aligned with design thinking methodology. For projects in which you anticipate using the Success Case Method from the beginning, telling learners you will be including their voice in evaluating the training can help drive buy-in or engagement in the process.

Work on Your Own

Think about a learning experience in which you participated. Reflect on the following questions, and document your answers in appendix 12.

- What activities occurred at each step of the learning journey, starting with learn?
- Which metrics might have been effective for evaluating the successful completion of the learning journey? (It is not necessary to have one for every step; decide which activities would yield the most meaningful data.)
- Refer to the LTEM model in appendix 11. Which tier does each metric correlate with?
- Study your completed evaluation plan. How might you adjust the learning experience if a metric fell below expectations?

Summary

Despite its value to a project, evaluation that goes beyond learner perception is rare. Hopefully this chapter provided a few ideas about how to begin doing evaluation activities that yield more results-oriented insights. Keeping the mindset of "designing for the journey" helps elevate the ultimate outcomes a learning experience is designed to achieve and encourages the project team to ensure that journey stays the course at each step along the way.

Now that we've covered the entire design process and all the steps in our LXD Framework, it's time to turn to selling your use case. In section 5, we'll discuss getting buy-in and how to start midstream as well as two case studies that show design thinking in action.

SELL YOUR USE CASE

11 Get Buy-in From Stakeholders

In This Chapter:

- What's different with design thinking?
- Strategies for getting access to learners
- How to deal with a hard "no"
- Getting buy-in for a new process

You've taken our four principles to heart, you're ready to put the tools to work, and now you have a project and a client ready to begin. As the requestor of a training solution, this client might be a department you support if you are internal to an organization, or someone inside a company, association, or not-for-profit organization if you are an external consultant. The stakeholders are all those with a vested interest in the outcome of the project and are the ones who will likely provide input into it.

As you get ready to kick off the project, the following questions may be nagging at the back of your mind:

- What, if anything, do you need to tell stakeholders up front about design thinking as a problem-solving strategy or specific tools or techniques you plan to use?
- How do you respond if they push back at specific points or to the overall concept?

The rest of this chapter is meant to answer these questions so you can feel confident getting started.

First, let's think about what and where you may make unique requests if you opt to use design thinking tools and processes. The client has already determined a perceived need and decided to apply resources to meet that need. What sets design thinking apart from a typical ADDIE or SAM approach? What you're asking for from your client that may be new or unexpected include:

Access to learners. Audience analysis is already an aspect of good instructional design. However, clients often perceive they've done it already or that subject matter experts are an acceptable substitute for actual target learners. They may even have reached out to target learners themselves and done a traditional needs analysis. Gaining learners' perspectives up front to verify the problem statement and provide perspective that informs design decisions is the biggest ask you have, and it can be one of the most challenging ingredients to get. This goes for learners who are employees inside your organization or customers outside it.

A different design and development process. We explained the training and development version of the design thinking process in chapter 3. It is compatible with other models, but it may add tasks or call for variations in how some things get done. Here's what may be new:

- engaging new stakeholders or engaging with existing stakeholders more frequently
- spending time on problem refinement and considering learner perspectives in refining that definition
- validating constraints rather than just accepting perceived constraints
- thinking beyond an "event" or a "course" to an entire learning journey
- taking time to gather learner perspective and formulating personas to shape design decisions
- ideating together rather than doing it independently and then returning to impress the client with your design savvy
- hanging in design-phase work longer by prototyping and iterating before moving forward to development
- incorporating actual learners in reviews and focusing feedback on how well the solution satisfies learner needs as well as business goals (and not just whether it has "right" content in it).

If you have a client who asks questions and wants to know the "why" on any or all these things, you need to be able to explain what you are doing and the value of it. In this chapter, we examine each of these two items and how to respond to questions your client may have about the requests you make.

Getting Buy-in to Include Internal Learners

In our experience, access to learners is the most common objection we face and have to address with clients. Yes, it is ironic that clients frequently push back on the request to include the perspective of the people for whom they are designing a solution. However, they often do it in a mistaken belief that they truly know what the learners want and need. These are the ones we hear a lot (Figure 11-1).

Figure 11-1. Common Objections to Internal Learner Access

When you hear these objections or similar ones, take a deep breath. Recognize that clients are not trying to be difficult. Their objections typically come from three places:

- **Belief that costs outweigh benefits.** To your clients, time is money; it costs a lot to pull people from their day job to spend time in perspective-gathering sessions and full-day design meetings. For example, a typical salesperson at Company X sells $2 million per year plus commission. Sales managers may not be thrilled to take away salespeople from selling for a day or two so they can help design learning solutions.
- **Belief that there is no benefit because they already know what's needed.** This one is common—and tough. Often people in a conference room determine what content is needed by learners. Perhaps these people once did the job of target learners. Perhaps they

manage the target learners. Or, perhaps, they are "content owners," who create the content that other roles need to learn. (Think of Marketing as the content owner of product and sales messages that salespeople use to sell.) The content owner often has never done the job of the learner—but has a lot of power in determining what and how the content gets taught.

- **Belief that it cannot be done—it's too much to coordinate or too big a hassle.** This one, too, is relatively common. Project timelines are routinely ridiculous and under-scoped. People are routinely over-committed. In some work environments, there are only a couple people capable of performing a particular role. Telling your client you need target learners to attend meetings or participate in other ways can sometimes be overwhelming. If they don't have ready access to learners themselves, they may be intimidated by trying to find you some target learners.

Let's look at three strategies to tackle each of these objections.

Strategy #1: Show Them the Money

Calculate costs and discuss costs versus benefits with them. We've included a cost analysis worksheet in appendix 13 to help you come up with a ballpark estimate of what it will cost to design and implement a learning solution. It often costs more than people think when you tally up people's time (internal soft costs) and the hard cost of paying external consultants.

Compare those costs to the desired benefit you hope to reap: increased revenue, decreased costs, reduction in turnover, increased speed to full productivity, or whatever number you are trying to nudge.

Ideally, you'll see that the benefit of the program dramatically exceeds the cost but only if the solution that gets implemented works.

Strategy #2: Gently Prod Assumptions

Discussing costs and benefits lets you have a conversation that gently inquires about assumptions and the risk of making them. You can go a step further and ask questions such as:

- If this training doesn't achieve the desired outcomes, what's the impact on you and the company given its approximate cost of $X to produce and implement it?
- What assumptions are you making about the learners' workflow, motivation to learn, thoughts and feelings, and daily experiences that have an impact on objectives we define, the content we include, or activities we design? Given what you are spending to create the training, is it beneficial for us to verify assumptions by involving learners or observing them?
- If we go with the assumptions of you or your stakeholders, what's the worst outcome that might happen if the assumptions are incorrect? Is that a risk you want to accept?
- How important do you think it is to fully understand what the learner is seeing and doing as they are supposed to use *[insert desired skill or knowledge]*? What about what they might be thinking or what their pain points and motivators are?
- How certain are you of the context—and the specific amount of time they may have—to use *[fill in the blank on skill or knowledge]*?
- Who on your team can speak to the workflow of the target learners and how this skill or knowledge needs to integrate with that existing workflow?
- Who can speak to what's actually realistic about the time these learners can make for this initiative—and where they might be when they have time to devote to it? (This goes to figuring out what tool is best as a delivery method, which isn't always the tool the client may want to use starting out.)

You might also have them try their hand creating an empathy map on behalf of the learner. As an effective eye-opener, we've posed the question: As learners use *[insert desired skills or knowledge]*, what are they:

- Thinking and feeling?
- Seeing and hearing?
- Saying and doing?

When stakeholders realize they cannot answer those questions, they often conclude that they should pull in some learners after all.

Once you get stakeholders a bit uncomfortable about the assumptions they are making—for the money they are spending—you may get a response such as, "OK. I see your point that learner perspective can really add value. But we truly cannot bring them in for a day." Or, "OK, I see your point, but I cannot pull together a ton of learners and arrange for you to talk with them."

Those kinds of comments lead us to the next strategy.

Strategy 3: Use Viable Alternatives to Minimize Time Requirements

Acknowledge the reality of limited bandwidth on the part of either learners or the client. Point out that it is still possible to gain valuable perspective from learners even if they cannot be physically present for the entire design meeting. Determine whether learners can call in for a portion of the design meeting and be available to provide feedback on the resulting design. If not, use observations, interviews, and focus groups to suit your needs.

You can minimize the client's effort in orchestrating interviews with internal (or external) learners by taking the following approach:

1. Give them a specific profile of who you'd ideally like to talk with. That profile will differ with each project, but consider attributes that you think will influence someone's perspective of a problem or an opportunity, such as: tenure in the position, tenure with the company, their level of career and role success, and their current knowledge or experience level with whatever your solution will address. Ideally you want people you think would champion the creation of your solution as well as a couple of detractors or skeptics.

2. Ask them to use this profile to generate a list of several target learners' names and contact info. If they need to reach out to others to get a list of names, provide verbiage they can use for that request. Make sure you have them collect names, emails, and phone contact info.

3. Once they assemble a list of names, provide your client with an email message that you've crafted on their behalf. That email will introduce you as well as the project and its goals. It will indicate that you will be contacting them to set up time to talk, visit, or whatever you intend. All your client needs to do is copy that text into an email and send it to those on the list of learners.

4. After the email goes out, you do the rest. You reach out, arrange for connections, and you are set up to gain valuable perspective you otherwise might not have received.

5. In our experience, most learners love being included in discussions about what to design and they have plenty to say. They are also equally delighted to give feedback on early prototypes or ideas, so be sure to ask what time and interest they would have in continuing to be part of the project. You will likely be delighted by what you hear from them, particularly if you make it easy for them to participate.

Get Real: Lack of Learner Access Blows Things Up

We were redesigning a large compliance curriculum for two broad audiences. It was a quick design phase—less design meeting time than we wanted, and no time to gather learner perspective prior to the meeting. The list of meeting attendees included the subject matter expert for each audience's compliance requirements. We convinced ourselves that while it was not ideal to not have any learners in the room, the subject matter experts must spend a lot of time with the target audience or they wouldn't understand the audience's daily tasks (and the compliance training the audience needs so they can perform those tasks in a compliant way). Sounds logical, right?

Wrong. We identified sub-audiences for each broad group but struggled to come up with job titles and responsibilities for each sub-audience profile. We got zero insight into any "day in the life" realities we hoped to better understand. Our goal going into the meeting was to redesign the training to make it more relevant, easier to access within the learners' workflow, and less time-consuming to complete. With no learner input, we were unsure whether we achieved those goals.

If we could redo the design meeting, we would do it differently. Instead of trying to use a design thinking approach without the right perspectives in the room, we would have played to the strengths of the people who were there and accepted that design thinking was not going to work in this project. We would have used experts' time to understand the content better, rather than try and extract learner perspective from people who didn't have it.

Lesson learned.

Getting Buy-in to Access Learners Outside the Organization

Sometimes the training solution you're developing is for people who are outside the client's organization, such as for customer education training. You're likely to receive similar objections to learner access (Figure 11-2). The same strategies you use for gaining access to internal learners often work here. The show me the money strategy is effective, as is focusing your client on the value of a well-crafted, targeted solution versus the risk of failure for a poorly targeted one. A well-done customer education program can be a differentiator that helps an organization become a market leader in a space. When customers spend significant dollars on a product, they expect world-class product training that minimizes loss of productivity. We've done several programs where the product being bought is a high-dollar one and the customer ramp-up time is a factor in the buying decision. In these instances, it is typically easy for clients to understand the upside of including customers in solution design and the risks of not doing it.

Figure 11-2. Common Objections to External Learner Access

On other types of projects, though, it can be tougher. If you try the preceding strategies and the client says, "I cannot or will not get you direct access," but they also acknowledge that perspective matters, ask for these things:

- **Voice of the Customer data.** Marketing or customer support functions may have this, particularly if they do any work with Net Promoter Score or other customer satisfaction survey tools.
- **Personas that were created by either a product development team or marketing function.** Teams in these areas often craft personas to help shape product design decisions or marketing messages that will resonate. There is a strong relationship between marketing and training. Both functions craft messages and experiences designed to change behavior.
- **Conversations with salespeople or customer support people who go on-site to customers** (or at least talk directly with them on a frequent basis) may give some high-quality second-person perspective. This is not an equivalent replacement for direct perspective, but it is better than no perspective from those directly interacting with the target learners.

Dealing With the Hard "No" to Access

Sometimes the project manager won't even consider learner inclusion, and the root cause could be anything from perceived clarity about the desired solution to a fear of negative comments from the target learner. You try, and the client is a solid brick wall with no entry anywhere.

If you have tried the strategies we've listed with no luck, you have a choice to make:

- **Proceed despite the risks.** Worst case scenario, the investment may not be an investment at all, but simply an expense as you yield no desired outcomes. Best case, you get some benefit but not as much as you might have.

- **Attempt to escalate.** If your client has a boss you think would be amenable to hearing your rationale for wanting to gain direct access to learners, you can try it. You may also push the decision if you perceive a great threat to the organization or to learners if you don't get perspective. If you opt for this choice, proceed with caution. Try to position yourself as an ally with the client as you work together to do what's best for the organization and the project. "How about I help you craft a presentation you can use to explain the value of learner perspective to your stakeholders—and the risks of not gaining that perspective. I'm happy to co-present with you if that would be helpful."

- **Gently decline to proceed.** Your ability to do this obviously depends on the power you have to say "no" and walk away. There is no judgment from our end if you opt to proceed anyway. We get the challenges. You may not win your battle, but if you do a good job of communicating risks you at least can go forward knowing you did your best.

If you decide to proceed, you can either continue trying to educate your stakeholders about the intended approach, or you can deviate from the design thinking approach at that phase of the project. Table 11-1 summarizes these two approaches.

Table 11-1. Two Approaches for Dealing With Hard "Nos"

	Educate: Persuade the stakeholders to follow your approach	Deviate: Propose an alternative method that provides similar outcomes
When to do it	• The client is interested in using design thinking or is open to it after you probed their assumptions. • You need to help make the case to other stakeholders on the project.	• The client has raised objections to your requests for learner or stakeholder involvement. • The scope or timeline of the project requires an alternate approach.
How to do it	• Check assumptions. • Do a cost analysis. • Show how design thinking principles can help maximize value of the final solution. • Identify where design thinking tools or techniques provide the biggest impact. • Inform the client about how the process or attendees you're requesting will impact the outcome.	Consider how you could accomplish your goals before or after you had originally intended. For example: • Collect learner data in advance via observations and interviews to share during the design meeting. • Circle back with learners or stakeholders who were absent from the meeting to confirm key assumptions or decisions in the design.

Share the Benefits of Design Thinking to Drive Buy-In

A common tenet of design thinking is "show don't tell." It is easier for someone to buy into a new approach when they can see what the process looks like rather than read bullet points in an agenda. We have assembled a short design thinking portfolio PowerPoint deck that shows rather than tells the benefits. It includes photos of design meetings and graphics of the outputs we generate so clients can see proposed processes in action.

When you are getting started with design thinking, try out the tools with your own team first or as a pilot project with a trusted client. Then, take pictures and document successes. Showing the final product alongside how you got there is powerful; you can see examples in the case study chapters. Feel free to use them as examples until you have your own.

Even before you have examples to share, however, you can offer up these reasons why a design thinking approach is worth trying:

- **To confirm agreement on the problem you're solving.** Imagine you have assembled all the "right" stakeholders for a new product launch design. Each stakeholder has brought certain assumptions with them about what the outcomes of the launch training will be and what the challenges for accomplishing those outcomes are. For example, the marketing manager wants sales reps following an approved script; the operations manager wants sales reps entering data accurately in the CRM tool; the product owner needs to meet the sales goal by the end of the year; and the sales rep wants to sell stuff that's easy to sell and tools and messaging that work within the context of the calls they make. A successful sales launch looks very different to each of those people. Design thinking can help uncover the assumptions that each one is bringing to the table. It may require a conversation about how to prioritize those needs, but better to have a measured conversation at the very beginning of the project than a frustration-fueled argument later when it's more difficult—and more expensive—to change course.

- **To include the content you didn't know learners needed as well as get rid of content they don't need.** This is probably the most consistent "win" we see, and it happens in one of two ways:
    - *Perspective gathering uncovers content learners need to successfully master the topic that would have otherwise been overlooked.* This happens for several different reasons. Obviously, having a detailed understanding of what content needs to be shared and how the learner will apply it on the job yields more relevant content selection. But maybe content owners assume certain content "goes without saying," or perhaps expert performers may have established best practices that would be helpful to a beginner but have gone undocumented. Whatever the reason, providing the right content is critical to the learner experience.

- *Perspective gathering indicates the need to increase or decrease the level of detail and complexity.* This happens when learner input challenges stakeholders' assumptions about the scope of what learners need to know. Imagine you're in the product launch design meeting when a sales rep speaks up: "We are drilled on the sales process from the first day of onboarding, and we use it every day. I don't need you to tell me how to use the sales messages, or where they fit in the process— that's what you pay me for. Just give me the bullet points and let me decide how to use them with my customers." Every stakeholder in the room heard him say that, and suddenly the learning solution took on a different identity, shifting from overly explained (and potentially condescending) to a quick or just-in-time reference. This leads to the next benefit.

- **To package content in the most usable and accessible format.** We were leading a design meeting for a large software training curriculum. There was only one learner in the room, and he didn't say a lot. But one comment we'll never forget: "I want it to be clear, easy, simple—one stop." That single comment catalyzed a conversation that led us away from 12 online modules toward a portal full of just-in-time video tutorials and job aids. It would have been a hard sell for us to pivot so dramatically based on our gut feeling about this, but driven by the learner himself, it was impossible for the stakeholders to ignore what was clearly a more usable solution.

- **To create solutions that live in the sweet spot, balancing the learners' and the organization's needs and constraints.** Imagine you have just launched a new online module. You've worked with the team for months to make sure all the content is signed off on by all necessary approvers, and now it's out there in the wild. Three months go by, then six. After 12 months you pull the analytics report. It's so sparse you are convinced you made an error. Of the hundreds of learners you sent this module to, only 60 ever opened it. Only 20 of the 60 viewed more than the first few pages, and less than 10 actually completed it. You do a quick tally and estimate that over $60,000 of resources were invested in developing and launching the module. Now instead of an analysis, you're doing a post-mortem, figuring out how to rebalance the learners' needs for access and brevity with the organization's needs for accuracy and legal approval. Design thinking helps prevent this scenario. Learners' perspectives clearly needed to be gathered before the decision was made to create a module only a tiny subset of learners completed.

- **To cultivate engaged, self-regulating stakeholders and subject matter experts.** Talent development professionals occasionally work with subject matter experts (SMEs) who do not understand the vision for the project. These SMEs frequently need to be asked, "Does the learner really need to know that?" or, "How would you explain that to a beginner?" Design thinking helps create alignment around the vision for where you're going so that everyone working on the project knows who the learner is, what level of information the learner needs, the context in which the learner will use the content from the training, and the outcomes it's driving toward. When the SME starts questioning themselves about "Does *[learner persona]* really need this? How will *[learner persona]* apply this?"—that's when you should feel confident that you are all rowing in the same direction.

Get Real: Discovering Buried Content

It doesn't take a room full of people to yield valuable content insights. We led a design meeting for a single online module with two subject matter experts, including one who was a former sales rep. We pieced together an empathy map as a bullet list of learner thoughts and characteristics. While asking about the learners we were really struck by one bullet point:

- Lots of competition for mindshare; sales rep gravitates toward simple or high-commission products.

It turns out the product we were designing the module about was neither simple nor especially commission heavy. Our immediate thought was, "Why on earth would the learner be motivated to sell this product?"

We posed this question to the stakeholders, who had not considered the question of motivation. After thinking about it, they explained the potential benefit: this product could open the door to other stakeholders at a customer site, especially ones whose sales opportunities were currently "maxed out."

Well—that's huge! Of course we made that point explicit in the training module. We're confident that the question of motivation would never have floated to the surface if we had not been focusing in detail on the learner's perspective and realities.

This project is a great example of why we're such advocates of doing whatever pieces of design thinking you can. In this case, we did one empathy map to create one learner persona, and if the only benefit was the addition of one (arguably critical) learning objective, that's a big win for the project.

Failure to convince a client to use design thinking in a project is not a personal failure; there are some projects in which it's far more productive to invest your energy differently. In our experience, difficult projects are often ones involving a certain level of fear in the core project team: fear of working with an external vendor, fear of time constraints, fear of subject matter experts' time commitment, preemptive fear of a lack of demonstrable results, and so on. While design thinking can sometimes help voice these concerns, it is not a panacea. In those cases, it's difficult to request resources you want without first addressing the needs or fears of the project owners. Sometimes—for example, when there is a fear of a lack of demonstrable results—addressing those fears can take the duration of an initial project before your "trust bank account" has enough credit to take risks together. Try to keep two things in mind:

- **Don't decide it's "all or nothing."** Don't abandon the entire design thinking philosophy just because you couldn't do all the perspective-gathering you wanted or the iteration you hoped to do. Instead, focus on integrating the four principles whenever possible.

- **At the end of the day, you can't care more about the project than the project owner does.** We are confident that a design thinking approach will improve the outcomes of many projects if you have the buy-in and partnership of the client. But your clients are the gatekeepers: if they decide they won't "go there" with you on a design thinking approach, don't force it. Use design thinking in projects where there is trust and partnership. Having some early wins will give you proven outcomes to share the next time you need to create buy-in.

Work on Your Own

Think about a learning project you worked on recently.

- To adopt a design thinking approach to that project, how would your process have changed? How would what you need from the stakeholders have changed? Take a moment to write down the requests you would have for the client.
- With that client in mind, how do you think they would respond to those requests?
- Which strategies or benefits mentioned in this chapter would resonate most with this particular client? Practice that strategy or response out loud.

Summary

Design thinking is not a one-man show. Getting the buy-in of the project team is critical for recognizing learning as a journey, getting perspective, finding and minding the sweet spot, and prototyping before you refine. This chapter discussed gaining buy-in at the start of the project; in the next chapter we discuss how to incorporate design thinking strategies into a project already in progress.

12 Using Design Thinking When a Project Is Underway

In This Chapter:
- Why design thinking is a mindset, not a process
- When you can use design thinking after a project starts

Design thinking is a mindset, not a process. There is no substitute for having target learners in the design meeting as you determine exactly what the learning experience is going to be. However, since design thinking is more about keeping a human-centered focus than it is about following a rigid process, it is never too late to adopt this frame of mind. Perhaps you read this book and want to put what you've learned into practice right away. Or maybe you were forced to deviate from your preferred approach early in the project and want to restore the focus on the learner. Whatever the reason, we applaud your effort. This chapter explores some post-design design thinking scenarios, but first, a few reminders to set the stage:

- **Set your sights on adopting our four principles.** By incorporating design thinking mid-stream, you may wonder if and when you are doing "enough" to get the learner experience right. The best benchmark for this question is proactive embodiment of the four principles we introduced in chapter 2:
  - **Principle 1:** Recognize learning as a journey. People don't learn from events; they learn from a multi-pronged experience that begins with them noticing a need to learn something and ends with consistent integration of the learning into their performance.

- **Principle 2:** Get perspective. Perspective is multi-faceted and includes the stakeholders' insights about the business needs and desired operational results, the learners' experience about what life is really like in their workspace, and both groups' input on assumed and actual constraints.
- **Principle 3:** Find and mind the sweet spot. Gaining perspective informs the best way to balance the needs of the business, needs of the learner, and the real constraints of the project. This is not a one-and-done activity; you must reference the perspective of the business and learners as you develop and refine your solution.
- **Principle 4:** Prototype before you refine. The best solution is typically not the first one you come up with. Be prepared to do quick and early prototypes, get feedback, and refine as you go.

- **Don't forget you're bringing a new key reviewer, the learner, into the process.** Based on those four principles, you can see that the number 1 priority when integrating design thinking techniques late in the game is getting the learner involved. This is no different from bringing any other key stakeholder into the process midstream, so you should expect that they will not agree with every decision that has been made so far. In fact, it's very possible that they will call into question the foundational assumptions of the project, so prepare yourself for that possibility.
- **Remember why you're doing this.** If you're like most of our clients, you're working on initiatives that can't afford to fail. For these types of needs, the risk of not achieving results is always greater than the risk of doing rework or incorporating additional review cycles. If integrating the learner into the development process is too high a risk, it should raise serious concerns about whether the team has prioritized getting it done over getting it done right, and why.
- **Embrace feedback.** When it comes to involving learners (or any mid-stream reviewer), the greatest fear is rework. It feels inefficient

and opens the door to new errors and inconsistencies. As designers and developers, we need to see feedback as the gift that it is: an opportunity to better understand the needs and wants of the users and business stakeholders. Feedback is inevitable, and it can happen in one of three ways: You solicit and receive feedback directly from the source; you receive indirect feedback from someone guessing what another stakeholder would say; or you receive feedback after the solution is launched, either direct from the user, or indirectly based on business metrics. We prefer the first way every time—it's much safer, cheaper, and more efficient.

Now that we are on the same page, here are some scenarios for incorporating a design thinking approach after a project is underway.

Using Design Thinking Post-Design Meeting

This is probably the most common scenario for incorporating a design thinking approach after the project start. Maybe learners were not available for the design meeting. Perhaps you were denied access to them for some reason, and your design is built largely on the assumptions of the stakeholder team. The good news is, if the design is the blueprint for your build, at this point you haven't broken ground yet—you could make any changes to that blueprint, and the added time and cost are minimal.

What to Do

You've already heard the business perspective; your first priority to find and mind the sweet spot (principle 3) is to gain the learner perspective.

Who? Now that you aren't asking for the commitment of an in-person meeting, you may have access to more learners. Be thoughtful about the mix of voices that can deliver the greatest value. For example, instead of asking for "five to seven account managers," consider whether there might be differences among new versus tenured account managers, or among account managers from different geographic sales regions. Where stakeholders may have provided initial input about where the greatest differences occur, this is your chance to put those assumptions to the test.

What? Your immediate need is for learner input on the design. This is not just a matter of "read this and tell me what you think." It's easy to lose sight of how much information sharing and decision making happens during the design meeting; anyone who wasn't there is missing a lot of context for the project. You can make this step vastly more valuable by doing two things:

- **Provide a project overview.** Ideally, this is a live conversation in which the learners can ask clarifying questions along the way. Give some background on the project goals and describe the major assumptions and decisions from the design meeting. If a live conversation is not an option, consider recording a video or screenshare where you talk through the highlights. It is tempting to incorporate the project overview into the design or convey it solely via email, but avoid doing so. The details of a learning experience design are better conveyed verbally and visually than solely in walls of text.

- **Specify what and how you want them to review.** Ask yourself where the greatest risks are in not having learner input. The top three areas typically include the content and objectives, the delivery medium, and the style or theme. If you have created a mockup or prototype, you may want an early reaction to the navigation or functionality. Help learners focus their review on these items by providing specific prompt questions like, "Do these instructional objectives cover all of the knowledge and skills a new account manager needs?" or "Given your day-to-day activities, is a web app the best format to make resources accessible?" "Does this content match your job realities?" Similarly, call out constraints that are non-negotiable so that learners know the true parameters of the project—this is how you'll find the sweet spot. For example, specify why certain decisions have been made. "Materials must be launched by the software go-live date in two months, so initial content only includes tasks for daily users." You can describe these types of constraints during the project overview conversation mentioned above.

A design blueprint (described in chapter 3) does not portray every detail of a solution. For example, the level of content presented or how a theme is executed across multiple solutions can be difficult to understand by reading the document. Just like it might be hard for you to know from an architect's blueprint how much elbow room you'll have in a bathroom shower, it may be hard for a reader to visualize every aspect of a learning experience. This difficulty matters because reviewing the design is not an all-encompassing stamp of approval. Instead, think of it as permission to proceed to the next step in the development process.

How? Unlike the design meeting, the review meeting for the design blueprint can happen virtually. However, virtual review does not equal independent review. We consider it a best practice for teams to review designs together. Hearing others' observations helps reviewers better understand the design, and disagreements and decisions can be handled quickly. You can let people do an initial review independently, but after everyone has a chance to do a solo review, arrange a joint review call or meeting in which all reviewers participate. This approach gives the core team a chance to hear why learners made the comments they did. As the designer, your role is to find and mind the sweet spot. This might mean challenging the assumptions of the project or finding new compromises. For example, let's imagine you are designing training for a software rollout. A key assumption is that the short go-live time frame means only basic, daily tasks can be taught. Learners review the design blueprint and comment that each type of daily user also has non-daily tasks they will need to know immediately. Now you have a good conversation! The sweet-spot solution could be a host of things, including:

- Backtracking in the design process to create multiple personas for the daily user roles and determine what the critical tasks are for each role. (What a great demonstration of the value learners bring to the design meeting!)
- Modifying the design for a phased rollout in which only certain users or roles are being trained on the new software at once.
- Creating "super users" in each area who will do one-on-one training for the non-daily tasks their role performs.

- Deciding the go-live date is somewhat arbitrary and can be pushed back a bit to allow training development of all essential tasks.

No single role can make that decision in a vacuum. Only through inclusive dialogue can you arrive at the right solution for the best results.

Worst Case Scenario

Let's play this out: The learners push back on the content or format in the design blueprint. While the high-level goals hold, the details behind them—and the way you intended to present the content—is not going to accomplish what you need it to. You're back at square one. What now?

- **Remember, the cheapest time to fail is now.** We know how deflating it can be for a design to fall flat. But you can't lose sight of the alternative: Imagine getting to the next milestone for the original design, and falling flat then. Or—gulp—getting all the way to the finish line. The fact is, until time travel is possible, the least expensive day to fail is today. Move forward, and don't make the same mistake twice.

- **Decide what works.** Save time at the end of the review call (or schedule a subsequent call dedicated to this purpose) to ask learners what does resonate with them. Their number 1 concern during design review—and rightly so—was likely to poke holes in what didn't hold water. Now that that task is done, ask them to change their lens to what does work. Use the "How might we . . . " problem reframing tool from chapter 4 to get people thinking about what can work instead of what the barriers are. In our experience, even the most scrutinized design blueprint is still recognizable in its second iteration. Stay curious. Keep asking questions to determine what assumptions are correct and which pieces of the design can stay.

- **Agree on what happens next.** Depending on the degree of "surgery" required for editing the design blueprint, it may be inappropriate to push forward to whatever your next milestone originally was. Keep the "prototype before you refine" mentality and ask what would provide a proof of concept of the design before you begin developing each part. For example, could you gather a focus group of learners to vet the legitimacy of new content you've included? Can you create mockups or wireframes of a new tool to gain buy-in from the learners and reassure the stakeholders, or use a flow diagram to map the intended user experience? Or is there some new prototype—like a content outline and wireframe hybrid—that helps visualize where you're going? This decision is going to be different for every project but warrants an intentional conversation to keep all team members engaged.

- **Document this situation in your portfolio!** Just as it can be helpful to show new stakeholders what good looks like when trying to explain design thinking, it can be just as eye-opening to describe what not-good looks like. Projects in which late learner input changed the course of the project are a testament to the value of learner involvement from the very beginning. Catalog these stories so you can share them with clients who may initially balk at backtracking. Stories are powerful motivators to help people see the value of actions.

Using Design Thinking During Development

You're knee deep in a project, but you are reading this book and want to put design thinking into practice right away. That's great! But you're wondering how. Here are a few suggestions to get started.

What to Do

As the project moves further and further into development, the landscape becomes increasingly complex. Suddenly there are more players on the team—SMEs, budget-holders, developers, reviewers—but as the designer, you are still leading everyone toward the desired results. It's time to meet your target learner (better late than never) to get perspective, find the sweet spot, and make sure you've designed an effective learning journey.

Who? One of the biggest challenges in switching to a learner-centered approach during development is bringing all the project's team members along with you. Developers and subject matter experts who have joined the project since the design phase all need visibility and agreement about the importance of a learner-centric approach. For large projects, this can be a lot of people.

What?

- **Create a learner persona.** The good news is, it's never too late to create a learner persona. This is an easy, non-threatening place to start, because by itself it has no impact on the product.

- **Map the learning journey.** How will learners notice and commit to learning about this topic? How will you provide practice and reinforcement? This is likely one of the greatest opportunities for enhancing the existing design. Make sure that each phase of the learning journey is accounted for in your design to ensure that learners apply new knowledge on the job and achieve the desired organizational results. Often, business stakeholders have not fully visualized what it is really going to take to go from event to business results. They find the journey eye-opening when you walk them through it—and show them where gaps exist.

- **Experience-map the desired learner experience.** Once all the elements of the learning journey are in place, create an experience map of the "future state." How does this experience align with the learner persona's day-to-day realities? Where are you being intentional about maximizing magical moments and minimizing miserable moments?

- **Decide what to prototype before fully developing.** If there are components that have not yet been created, consider what a minimum viable product could look like to confirm with learners and business stakeholders that the solution will be effective as designed.

- **Incorporate user testing.** The thought of user testing can be intimidating, conjuring up pictures of eye tracking software and metric dashboards. The fact is, simply sitting next to someone using your solution while they think out loud can provide invaluable insight.

How? In this case, the "how" is two-fold: how to execute the activities above, and how to make meaning of them with your project team. Since we have detailed how to do the activities in previous chapters, let's talk about how to gain buy-in with your team.

It is important to note, if there is such a thing as meta-design-thinking, this is it: You are managing the project team's experience while asking them to manage the learner's experience. You'll need to wear two hats to gain the team's perspective while finding and minding the sweet spot. It's no small task, to be sure, but worth it in the end.

With that in mind, the key is to involve team members as the project allows to create the persona, learning journey, and so on. Then, let the team decipher what these mean to their roles on the project. You might pose questions to help get the conversation started, such as:

- (To developers) "How does the persona inform your vision of the end result?"
- (To SMEs) "What does the persona tell you about the level of content we should be targeting?"
- (To learners, SMEs, and business stakeholders) "Where during the learning journey do we run the most risk of learners 'opting out' of the experience, and what impact will that have on our results?"

The simple act of asking team members to draw their own conclusions (and adjust accordingly) helps foster ownership of the learner experience across the team.

Get Real: Mapping the Journey Post-Design

We met with a client recently to help design post-event reinforcement for a complex curriculum. The organization was launching a new product, and because of the anticipated sales increase, they were simultaneously hiring about 250 new sales reps that had to be fully onboarded into a highly regulated industry in about two months' time. The client team was motivated but understood the immensity of their challenge.

We had not been involved in designing the onboarding or product training—we were only there to assist with reinforcement. But we took the opportunity to step back and map the learning journey that was already in progress. Seeing all the activities plotted out that way was reassuring to them—it was a relief to visualize how they had accounted for each step of the journey relatively well to that point. It also highlighted how a communication campaign could help highlight where learners were at in that journey, reinforce where they had been, and explain what was coming next.

As we began designing reinforcement, having that conversation while looking at the learning journey map helped guide the timing and content to include in the solution. This example emphasizes why the four principles are mindsets, not activities.

Worst Case Scenario

Once again, the most painful consequence of involving learners at this point in the game is getting their feedback. If that's the case, remember the reason you thought it was a good idea in the first place: you wanted to find the sweet spot, the solution that meets the needs of the learner and the organization while abiding by the constraints of the project. Look at the learner feedback through your "sweet spot lens" to decide what to do with it. If the feedback points out disconnects in what is learned or how it is accessed, it might be worth the re-work cost versus the prospect of poor outcomes.

The silver lining of doing user testing is the opportunity to create buy-in to a new solution before it's launched. Just as having someone review your book before it's published engages them in potentially buying and promoting it, strive to create advocates by keeping testers in the loop about how their feedback impacts the final product. When it comes to launching new training solutions, positive word of mouth is like a pot of gold at the end of the rainbow.

Using Design Thinking at Pilot

It is still possible to use design thinking when you have pilot-ready instructor-led training (ILT) materials or beta e-learning materials that have been developed completely and undergone two rounds of review. While this is technically part of the development phase detailed above, we call this scenario out specifically because post-pilot or launch-ready materials are often turned around very rapidly after the pilot is complete. In other words, the pilot is very near the end of the project. So why even consider incorporating a human-centered perspective at this point? Because it can save you from rolling out a "solution" that won't get you the results you need or intend.

What to Do

The purpose of a pilot is to validate that the activities, materials, timing, and flow of the workshop all work as intended. To do that, you need an audience. What an opportunity to bring in target learners!

While you have learners in the same room together, consider what other information might be helpful to gather perspective. Consider creating an experience map of the magical and miserable moments during the pilot. Even if your pilot materials are right on target, this is a perfect time to consider the learning journey beyond the single event. Get learners' input on what comes next, when they want it, and the best format for that solution.

Worst Case Scenario

As you get later and later in the project, there's more at stake, so you have to look through a sweet spot lens that's progressively more critical. At this point, when it comes to negative feedback, the questions to ask yourself are:

- What would it mean if I got this feedback from participants during the session?
- What would it mean if I got this feedback from participants in session evaluations?
- What would it mean if I got this feedback from a business stakeholder after the session?

If the answer to one of those questions is uncomfortable and not one you want to live with, make the change. Consider yourself lucky to have received the gift of feedback before you could no longer make changes.

Of course, when big changes are involved, it's ill-advised to charge headlong into the session launch. Take a moment to discuss what the appropriate next milestone is. Consider scheduling a walk-through meeting or web conference once changes are implemented or sending screenshots of new material for approval before going to print. It likely doesn't require another pilot session, but a quick run-through can save a lot of stress and cost.

Using Design Thinking to Revise an Existing Project

Perhaps as you've read this book, you have been thinking of a project that you wish had included a design thinking approach. Or maybe one of your projects is ready for scheduled maintenance, and you're wondering if there is a way to look at it with fresh eyes. Happily, there is a structured way to adopt a design thinking approach in either scenario.

What to Do

Unlike some of the other scenarios in this chapter, when a solution is already out in the world, perspective-gathering is not your first task. To identify enhancements that will make an impact on desired outcomes, you must first go back to square one to confirm the team's agreement on what the original need was. A strategy blueprint from chapter 4 can help organize this discussion.

Clarify the challenges you'd hoped to resolve and measurable outcomes you hoped to achieve. While it's hard to "un-know" what the existing program includes, try to approach this step as though there isn't a program in place. Remember, you're not looking to confirm everything in the current program, you want to stay honest about what can be improved. A stakeholder who has limited familiarity with the program can be a valuable asset to help preserve objectivity.

Evaluate the existing program against the identified outcomes. Depending on what metrics the program was intended to achieve, this might be as easy as looking at pre- and post-event data, or it might require interviews with managers to confirm how behaviors are being applied on the job. Fair warning: Ancillary data is likely to arise during this process that informs or distracts from the outcomes data. For example, you could discover:

- Usage data shows that only 10 percent of learners completed the first module, meaning the current program has no hope of meeting the result metrics.
- Only a few managers have rolled out training to their teams; the majority do not intend to roll out until the next fiscal year.

- The Asia-Pacific region completed training on hiring practices but has not had an opportunity to implement because of an extended hiring freeze.

Despite these types of realizations, remember your goal: to evaluate how well the program in question solved the original problem. If possible, it is still worthwhile to see if you can pro-rate the outcomes for learners who completed the program and had opportunity to apply it.

Gather perspective to better understand use case and implementation gaps. Don't assume you know exactly why learners are or aren't accessing and applying training on the job. Keep principle 2, *get perspective,* in mind as you learn about the experience directly from the learners. Here are a couple ways to do that:

- **Create a learning journey map of the current learning experience.** How is each phase accounted for? Talk to learners to find out what would be most useful to them in each phase. In the spirit of "prototype before you refine," consider how you might prototype any new aspects of the learning journey before rolling it out to all learners.
- **Create an experience map (with learners) of each phase of the learning journey to better understand the high and low points.** This is a great way to check your assumptions about how learners notice and commit to the experience, how the experience fits into their workflow, and when and how learners apply new skills on the job.

Finally, here are some questions to consider where the learning experience might fall short:

- Are the right learners accessing this resource at the right times?
- Do learners receive the information and practice they need to be successful on the job?
- How is on-the-job performance supported and reinforced?
- How are learners motivated or engaged throughout this process?

Worst Case Scenario

Much like the previous scenarios in this chapter, the worst-case scenario is that you discover a current solution is ineffective as-is. When that happens, take time to identify what is working, and include target learners and relevant stakeholders in defining the changes that best complete the learning experience. From that point, you are basically jumping into the ideate step of the LXD framework.

Make sure you document these kinds of stories in your design thinking portfolio! Projects that are forced to pivot are not failed programs; they are evidence of your team's conscientious alignment to business goals.

Work on Your Own

Think of one project that is already in progress or even already launched. Use the strategies defined in this chapter and fill in the template in appendix 14 to create a step-by-step action plan for using design thinking techniques within that project.

Summary

Throughout this book, we've tried to send the message that design thinking doesn't have to be all or nothing, and even small perspective-gaining activities can yield pivotal insights. Hopefully you feel empowered to start small, whether that's an empathy map for a just-getting-started project or user testing on an almost-fully-developed solution.

13 CAISO Scheduling Coordinator Curriculum

In This Chapter:

- Background on CAISO
- The process with an empathy map and a persona
- The results

This project occurred just as we began exploring the process and benefits of design thinking. At that point, our focus was on validating whether empathy maps and personas were worth the time they took at the beginning of a project. As you can probably guess, this was one of the projects that encouraged us to dig deeper into design thinking and what it could do to transform the design process.

Background

The California Independent System Operator (CAISO) is a nonprofit public benefit corporation that manages the flow of electricity across the high-voltage, long-distance power lines that make up 80 percent of California's power grid. As the only independent grid operator in the western United States, CAISO grants equal access to nearly 26,000 circuit miles of transmission lines and co-ordinates energy resources into the grid. It also operates a competitive whole-sale power market designed to promote a broad range of resources at lower prices: every five minutes, CAISO forecasts electrical demand and dispatches the lowest cost generator to meet demand while ensuring enough transmission capacity for delivery of power. You can imagine that an organization with such a crucial role in the region has low tolerance for error.

To participate in the CAISO market, a company must achieve certification as a scheduling coordinator (SC). This certification allows them to buy or sell energy in the market and handle the settlements process after the market closes. The live multi-day certification workshops are held three to four times per year and are only open to entities on track to become scheduling coordinators. This created a couple of pain points:

- **Accessibility.** Attendees are given print copies of the content, but if someone from the SC did not attend the live workshop, there was no way to access the information from those sessions. The presentations were not available online. If someone wanted information about the day-ahead market, for example, content is available elsewhere on the website if the learner was motivated to search for it. And that search is no small task: as we began researching content ourselves, we realized how much content existed on the website. The vast content library was great but could make it difficult to find exactly what you need.

- **Availability.** Many of the foundational topics covered in the certification training are applicable to other customers as well, but for these other customers to access them, they needed to enroll in a separate multi-day workshop. There was an opportunity to create efficiency in delivering these foundational topics.

Our Design Workshop

The two-day design workshop included nearly 30 people, a mix of internal stakeholders, subject matter experts, and members of scheduling coordinator entities. That's a lot of people! Because of the highly technical nature of the subject matter, staff develop narrow, deep expertise in a specific area. Some of the attendees were there to provide expertise in only one of the 20-some initial topic areas. For this project, getting their initial buy-in at the beginning of the project was important, for reasons you'll read about later in this chapter.

Empathy Map

We began by creating a simple learner profile. Her name was Linda; she was 30 years old, with a bachelor's degree in accounting, and brand new to her organization. That was it—from there we began empathy mapping to create a shared appreciation of the day-to-day realities of our learner. Here are a few direct quotes from the empathy map we created that day (Figure 13-1):

- **Thinking:** "I really can't afford to make a mistake." "Where do I start?"
- **Feeling:** Intimidated, overwhelmed.
- **See:** A myriad of "supposed" links and sites.
- **Hear:** Siloed messaging; "Don't call this person, call that person."
- **Say and Do:** "A normal day is a good day—a thousand 'atta-boys' don't make up for one 'uh-oh.'" "I've heard different stories about how this situation should be handled." "This is cool!"
- **Pains:** Training is done by the current employee in that role; Linda picks up that person's processes as well as their bad habits. Linda is an hourly employee, without time allotted for training activities.
- **Gains:** Challenging work; likes to learn new things; job security.

As part of the conversation, we also uncovered that we had been making a false assumption: Because "scheduling coordinator" sounds like a job title, we had conceptualized this label as a single person within a "scheduling coordinator" organization. And, to be fair, that may be the case at small scheduling coordinator organizations. But for most of these organizations, responsibilities are split between multiple Lindas. This was a pivotal discovery, because it sparked the need to define task categories and a corresponding learning pathway for each one. That allowed a Linda who was only responsible for certain tasks to only take the relevant training modules, instead of requiring everyone to take every module. As a result, we created four learning paths (Figure 13-2). Because our Linda empathy map did not include task-specific information, there was no need to create multiple empathy maps or personas.

Figure 13-1. Empathy Map for "Linda"

Figure 13-2. Four Learning Pathways Based on Task Categories

Updated SC CBT Course Paths

	Load	Supply in ISO BA	Interchange resources	Financial Partcipants
ISO Orientation	1	1	1	1
Day-Ahead Overview	2	2	2	2
Real-Time Overview	3	3	3	3
Emergency Response	4	4	4	
Master File Process		5	5	
Interchange and e-Tagging Market Award			6	
Outages Overview		6		
OMS Basics		OMS Users		
OMS Advanced		OMS Users		
AIM	AIM Users	AIM Users	AIM Users	AIM Users
Metering Overview	5	7		
Settlements Process	6	8	7	4
Commitment Costs	7	9	8	
Settlements Validation	8	10	9	5
Settlements Validation Practice	9	11	10	6
MRI-S	MRI-S Users	MRI-S Users	MRI-S Users	MRI-S Users

Learner Persona

Our understanding of Linda painted a picture of a steep learning curve and a high-pressure work environment. After the design meeting, we constructed a persona to bring her to life (Figure 13-3).

Figure 13-3. Learner Persona for "Linda"

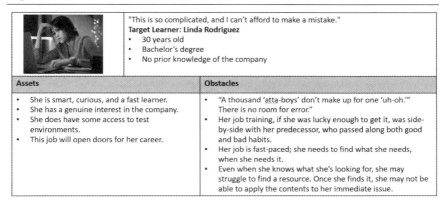

As we mentioned, we were just starting to explore design thinking tools; you can see that the persona is based almost entirely on key points from the empathy map. We did not do any observation, experience mapping, or day-in-the-life documentation, which we almost certainly would do today. However, Linda's impact on the project was only just beginning.

Where Did Linda Go?

One of the primary reasons we wanted to include this project as a case study is because it demonstrates how it's not about doing a persona for the sake of having a persona, but what you do with the persona that makes a difference.

The CAISO program manager deserves all the credit for what happened next. Since most of the content collection sessions and review meetings were scheduled to take place in the same conference room, she posted Linda's persona in the room, literally giving the learner a seat at the table as the modules were being built. As an external vendor, we rarely have visibility to those types of opportunities, so this "adoption" of Linda was an unanticipated but big win for the entire project team.

The other place Linda routinely showed up was in our content collection documents. The development team partnered with CAISO to provide a consistent format and process for collecting content for each module. In each one, Linda appeared at the very beginning as a reminder of the level of information the module should include (Figure 13-4).

Figure 13-4. Excerpt From a Content Collection Slide Deck

⟶ Don't forget Linda!

When you provide content, please think of our target learner: **Linda Rodriguez, who has no prior knowledge of CAISO.**

Be sure to include only what Linda needs to know, and explain it in language she would understand.

Assets

- She is smart, curious, and a fast learner.
- She has a genuine interest in the CAISO.
- She does have some access to test environments.
- This job will open doors for her career.

Obstacles

- "A thousand 'atta-boys' don't make up for one 'uh-oh.'" There is no room for error."
- Her job training, if she was lucky enough to get it, was side-by-side with her predecessor, who passed along both good and bad habits.
- Her job is fast-paced; she needs to find what she needs, when she needs it.
- Even when she knows what she's looking for, she may struggle to find a resource. Once she finds it, she may not be able to apply the contents to her immediate issue.

These activities had two primary effects:

- **Buy-in from the project team.** Recall that the subject matter experts (SMEs) had deep expertise on a specific topic. That meant that most modules had a unique SME; there were very few SMEs who informed more than one module. As a result, a given SME may not be called upon for this project until six months after they attended the design meeting. That's why it was so wonderful that most SMEs had attended that meeting—each of them had awareness and buy-in of the learner persona, meaning the program manager's burden of onboarding them to the project was minimized.

- **Self-regulating content owners.** Any time SMEs have deep knowledge about their topic, it's difficult for them to self-regulate what is and is not relevant to a particular learner or which concepts are simple versus complex. For this project, when SMEs started going into deep detail, the CAISO program manager was able to point back to Linda to say, "This person doesn't need to know everything you know." That was often all it took to refocus the conversation back to the right level. Sometimes, SMEs would even catch themselves going beyond the "Linda-sphere," a mindset which is mutually beneficial for the project team and for the learner.

An interesting fact that the program manager noted was the lifespan of the persona. Linda was helpful long after the content collection phase of the project. Often, review meetings would reopen content discussions about what or how much information to include about a particular topic. Linda was a valued reference point even as late as alpha reviews, which were the third iteration of the module SMEs had seen.

Results

At this point in our design thinking journey, we would have been happy if the only effects of the empathy map and persona were stakeholder buy-in and simplified content collection. Instead, we were pleasantly surprised to realize additional positive outcomes both for the learner and for the client organization.

Learner-Facing Impact

The final curriculum included a total of 23 resources across the four learning paths shown in Figure 13-2. They represented four different types:

- reference resources (administrative topics)
- foundational topics (concept-based)
- application topics (software)
- sustainability resources (reinforcement).

That was significant because the original scope of the project did not include any plans for reinforcement, and the reference topics had evolved during design as well. We realized that such a breadth and depth of content combined with Linda's need for quick access implicated some kind of "breadcrumbs" solution. That may sound obvious in hindsight, but as we were writing the design, we were agonizing over how to avoid "ditching" Linda after dropping 20 modules in her lap, and how to give her an optimal way to find and reference information that she had seen somewhere along her learning path.

Here were the implications for the format of the solutions:

- **Enable reference on any device.** Reference resources included administrative topics a learner might reference at any time during their training sequence, and would likely reference repeatedly. For these, we used an authoring tool designed to optimize responsiveness on any device or screen size.

- **Include accessible reinforcement.** For the reinforcement solution, we had two goals: make learners aware of the available topics and make it easy to locate key content. To accomplish these goals, we designed a responsive resource library: a mobile-friendly collection of animations, definitions, and examples about key concepts, with a hyperlink to the original module in which they appeared. The guide also housed a list of common questions and challenges, with links to associated modules, sections of the *Business Practice Manual*, and other resources or contacts useful for solving the issue.

Organizational Impact

In a company whose use of online training had been limited, the program manager still gets positive feedback from internal stakeholders. There are several benefits that the organization has realized:

- **Time and cost savings.** The original goal of delivering training that was more cost effective and more widely available was met.

- **Accessible support.** Historically, training session attendees received a print copy of the content; those who didn't attend were not able to access the same materials. Today, not only can learners access the materials, but they can revisit them as many times as necessary from one easily accessible page on the website.

- **Use of online training as customer support.** The program manager reports that the online modules have also proved useful as a customer support tool. While not the originally intended purpose, making the modules easily accessible on the website means that a broader population of internal and external learners can benefit from the project.

- **Use of online training as part of a blended learning strategy.** The foundational modules now available online cover a wide range of content. CAISO is able to use this content as prerequisites for the workshops to make better use of face-to-face training time for in-depth application.

The scheduling coordinator curriculum has been such a success that at the time of publication, CAISO is considering a second certification curriculum to realize some of the very same benefits: a more efficient delivery model for CAISO and a more personalized learning path for the learner.

Summary

This case study is not included as an example of "do everything we did for curriculum perfection!" If we started this same project today, we would likely make some different choices: We would certainly strive for more in-depth perspective gathering. We might reimagine how we planned for the first set of deliverables to allow for user testing. And we would try to build in an evaluative checkpoint after the first few modules launched to allow for any necessary course correction. So no, we didn't include this case study because it was perfect in every way; we included it because it's perfect in the ways that matter when you're just getting started with design thinking: We got out there and tried it. We had an ideal, collaborative client partner. We made the most of the tools we used. And we built upon the lessons we learned to bring with us into the next project, and the project after that.

As you get started using design thinking, don't feel like you must go all-in; pick a couple principles or tools to adopt, and just see what happens. Build in time to proactively discuss your observations and conclusions. For us, during the first few months of design thinking exploration our goal was just to learn something from every project about how and when to use the tools. Then we'd pause, draw some conclusions, and apply those best practices as we began adopting another tool. The NxStage case study shows how that process matured over time, allowing us to be more and more focused on the business problem, learner experience, and usability of the solution.

NxStage

In This Chapter:
- Background on NxStage
- A new problem for NxStage's training
- The design process

In some projects you get the opportunity to start the way you want to go. In the case of NxStage, a manufacturer of hemodialysis equipment, the entire project used a design thinking approach. We started with problem definition and used almost every technique we describe in this book. This chapter highlights what we did and the outcomes we achieved by using a design thinking approach. It's also something we've now done twice. The first time was in 2009-2010. The more recent time was in 2019.

Let's start with a bit of background on NxStage and its product and then we'll we dive into the project.

Background

NxStage invented a hemodialysis machine that was approved for home use in 2005. It was first to market in the home hemodialysis space. The introduction of NxStage's product into the marketplace offered an exciting alternative for kidney patients. With more frequent home hemodialysis, patients may see a reduction in the amount of toxin and water build-up between treatments. This may reduce or even eliminate the many side effects patients experience with conventional three-times-weekly therapy. In addition, with the NxStage machine, patients could do the dialysis in the comfort of their own homes.

The challenge is that it requires commitment and a positive attitude to learn how to do it. It can be intimidating to learn because patients must learn how to "self-cannulate." The cannula, which goes into the patient's arm vein, is what allows blood to flow from the patient, filter through the hemodialysis equipment, and then be pumped back into the body. An entire treatment cycle takes about four hours. Patients must connect themselves to the machine (or have a caregiver help), monitor the machine during its filtration process, and disconnect from it when the process is complete. They must troubleshoot problems with their machines, which can be a bit nerve-wracking until patients gain confidence with the error codes. They also must maintain their equipment and supplies. This translates to lots of knowledge and skill to acquire.

The therapy was a great alternative for patients, but NxStage was challenged in getting it to gain traction. After four years on the market, only 1 percent of the market was using the NxStage home hemodialysis product. NxStage believed the market could expand to 10-15 percent if they could eliminate the bottleneck related to training new patients on how to use the equipment. Training patients is far more labor- and time-intensive for home hemodialysis than it is for peritoneal dialysis. When NxStage approached Bottom-Line Performance (which is now TiER1 Performance Solutions) to help them solve their training bottleneck, these things were true:

- On average, it took 18 days (97 hours) to train a patient on how to do home hemodialysis using NxStage equipment. This translated to an average of 3.5 weeks of calendar time. In contrast, it took a nurse trainer about 38 hours to train a patient to do home peritoneal dialysis.

- Training needed to be done on a one-on-on basis: one nurse to one patient. A training day is typically 4.5 to five hours, which means the nurse typically trained only a single patient during a 3.5-week period.

- Reimbursement rates for training were extremely low. There was little incentive for a dialysis center to want to train patients in home hemodialysis (reimbursed at about 5 percent of actual cost) when they could train patients in peritoneal dialysis and receive much higher reimbursement (35 percent of actual cost).

In 2010, Bottom-Line Performance partnered with NxStage to create a training program for nurse educators in dialysis centers to alleviate this bottleneck and help improve metrics in two areas: patients who could be trained at any one time in-center and patient drops post-training. NxStage also wanted to create a scalable, repeatable training process that was easily learned and replicated so that nurses want to provide the training and patients find the training to be engaging and easy to follow.

To get started, we followed a traditional ADDIE-style analysis. We interviewed training nurses (home program nurse educators) as well as NxStage personnel. We observed training at a couple of dialysis centers. We reviewed data that NxStage provided. Then we pulled together a variety of people (nurse educators as well as NxStage personnel) and created an experience map (though we didn't call it that back in 2010 when we did the first project's design work). That experience map was an epiphany for every participant in the room. With it, everyone could clearly see that patients received way too much content in the first five to eight days of a four-week training cycle. There was also minimal to no repetition (except for the equipment and cannulation) of a lot of it. This lack of repetition increased the effort required by patients to learn and retain the information. It also contributed to longer training processes.

We used our findings and insights to come up with a program, called NxSteps, that included:

- A nurse trainer flipbook-style guide that enabled nurses to have their notes facing them while the other side of the flipbook was patient-facing.
- Several short e-learning modules for patients (this was in pre-mobile times so modules had to be viewed on a PC).
- Numerous quick-reference guides (QRGs) that were topically designed and included lots of images and white space with easy-to-read, simply written text. These QRGs focused on one key skill per guide, such as keeping things clean or troubleshooting.

Figure 14-1 shows some of the pieces of the toolkit.

Figure 14-1. NxSteps Materials

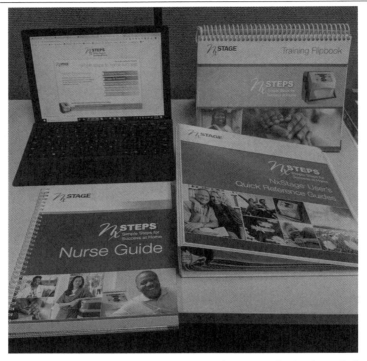

These were print-based for nurses and a combination of print-based plus e-learning modules for patients.

Keep in mind as we continue our story that something very key happened in January 2010: the iPad launched in the market. We pondered its usage as part of our design process, but the technology was too new. It had not reached critical mass, and WiFi at hemodialysis centers was extremely rare. We made the difficult decision that we needed to stay with print-based materials and couple them with e-learning modules that patients could access on desktop or laptop computers.

After eight months in development and the creation of an implementation strategy that leveraged some of the tools identified in chapter 10, NxStage launched its new training program. It was an immediate success. After the first year, the feedback was extremely positive, and the business goals were on track. Nurses using the NxStage materials loved them; patients undergoing the program were staying on therapy.

A New Problem

Fast forward five years, and different problems emerged. Program usage plummeted with these issues front and center:

- Nurses who had initially been appreciative of the detailed nurse binder, flipbook, and handouts no longer wanted such a large variety of materials to use for training. The print-based materials and bulky binder didn't lend themselves to customization by patient. It was cumbersome for nurses to customize the training approach or lessons to fit specific patient types (those who already knew how to self-cannulate versus those who did not, for example). As a result, the materials were being abandoned by nurses.
- The print Quick Reference Guides also weren't being used. After the implementation plan NxStage executed in 2011 ran its course, there was no longer a prioritized effort to educate new nurse educators on the materials or how to best use them. As nurse turnover occurred within dialysis centers, new nurses were unaware that NxStage materials even existed. Centers didn't want to have to reorder as supplies ran out. Nurses also weren't directing patients to the e-learning, with many centers not even having computers available for patients to use during their dialysis time. (The availability of computers in centers was identified as a possible constraint back in 2010, but the extent to which this was a problem was dramatically underestimated.) Patients often did not have the means to do the e-learning at home due to lack of computer access.

As the training materials were abandoned, NxStage needed to regroup. Its hemodialysis machine still had a life-changing therapy, but it once again needed to revisit the training approach and tools.

The Process

In early 2018, NxStage approached Bottom-Line Performance about reimagining its training. Early advantages the program provided back in 2011 when NxStage launched its training were no longer there. Mobile technology, pervasive Wi-Fi connectivity, and responsive design had changed the landscape in which training gets delivered.

While we conducted a robust analysis as part of the ADDIE framework in 2010, we shifted in 2018 to a human-centered design approach. This shift meant we focused heavily on usability from both the patient and nurse perspective and not just instructional goals. We involved patient advocates (people who use NxStage hemodialysis but are also paid by NxStage to support other patients in therapy) and nurse educators in info gathering and design sessions where they could do empathy mapping and listen to each other's experiences. We mapped out the learning journey from each vantage point: the nurse and the patient. We identified the miserable moments for each user (nurse and patient) and figured out how to fix them.

Here are key tools and processes we used and what we gained from them.

Initial Perspective Gathering and Analysis

Before we came together for a design workshop, we gathered initial perspective via several tools. In traditional ADDIE we would have focused on skill and knowledge gaps. With a design thinking hat on, we wanted to go beyond that to noting what the experience of learning dialysis is like and what makes it better or worse for a patient and a caregiver.

Table 14-1 identifies tools we used to prepare ourselves for a design meeting with patients and nurse educators as well as NxStage staff members.

Table 14-1. Tools Used During Design Meeting

Perspective-Gathering Tool	Insights Gained
Existing survey data (including NPS feedback and past site visit notes) and additional training plan for home hemodialysis from the UK	We gained a clearer understanding of the current training material, as well as a picture of training in the UK. This initial information assisted us in forming specific questions for the focus groups, surveys, and observations.

Perspective-Gathering Tool	Insights Gained
Observations and interviews with nurses and patients in-center for training	The paper tools appeared to require significant navigation effort on the part of nurses.
	Nurses we observed did not use the guides and relied on their prior experience instead. Instruction was lecture-based rather than the hands-on practice approach outlined in the NxSteps materials.
	Patients accessed and referred to their print materials during treatment setup but did not explore materials during treatment. Instead, they used their mobile phones for entertainment. They did not use tablets during training or treatment except as part of treatment monitoring with the NxStage Nx2me app.
	Both nurses and patients expressed a need for the training to remain a face-to-face experience, with observed practice.
Interviews with NxStage clinical consultants and stakeholders	These individuals all observed that nurses have an abundance of tools, and content within the tools can become quickly outdated. Clinical consultants shared in the focus groups that between 40 and 90 percent of their centers use NxSteps, but only 10-305 of that number use the materials as-is.
	In addition, from NxStage's perspective, the print materials require significant effort to update and distribute.

Table 14-1. Tools Used During Design Meeting (cont.)

Perspective-Gathering Tool	Insights Gained
Interviews with patient advocates	Patients shared that larger paper manuals were unwieldy during treatment. They indicated they frequently use their phones during treatment but were less likely to use tablets or laptops because of the size of those devices.
	They talked about some of the common medical complications—a general feeling of being unwell while going through training. They also revealed a need for larger font to make reading anything easier.
	Finally, the group was very willing to share ideas for content for a training app. They discussed features related to alarms and topics related to travel planning and supplies that build on previous NxSteps materials.
Surveys with patients and nurses	Survey data revealed some basic demographic information about patients. It confirmed access to Wi-Fi or cellular data service. It also revealed interest in some proposed training features for patients.
	The nurse survey also generated a list of nurses' ideal features. It too confirmed available technology and WiFi support. Finally, it validated the existing training topics from the original NxSteps curriculum.

These findings allowed us to create empathy maps, learner personas, and other critical components to use in the design meeting.

Table 14-2 shows implications from the analysis that influenced the app design.

Table 14-2. The Design Implications From Perspective Gathering

Finding	Design Implication
Though technology may be used, this training remains a face-to-face, hands-on experience.	In addition to any new tools like an app, the previous patient print tools should remain as both patients and nurse educators see a real value in them.
Patients and care partners are mostly looking for resources to use when home. Their vision for an app includes features that help them troubleshoot and complete other key tasks when their nurse isn't present. By contrast, nurse educators are looking for an option to use with patients during the training sessions.	Based on these different use cases, we recommend two separate apps based on audience.
Patients and nurses use a wide variety of technology, so an app must be able to respond to different tools ranging from a laptop to a phone.	Based on this and other constraints we've uncovered, we strongly recommend designing a responsive web app that allows cross-device use.
Use of NxSteps materials varies significantly. Several nurse educators do not use their Nurse Guide, the key tool that helps pull all the rest together. Various factors contribute to why nurses select which tools, ranging from personal preference to the training and support offered by clinical consultants.	To create a consistent experience, we recommend the nurse educator app drive all other training materials..

Our Design Workshop

This workshop continued the perspective-gathering process and then allowed us to ideate possible solutions. We didn't just want to talk about skills and knowledge; we wanted to map out the optimal experience for nurses and patients.

The Beginning of the Day: Empathy Mapping and Personas

We started with empathy mapping and persona creation. Based on our findings from the analysis work, we created an initial empathy map from the interviews and open-response results to the survey that we shared with key NxStage stakeholders to validate. From this map, we generated a detailed starter persona for both a patient and a nurse. Figure 14-2 shows the patient version. As a reminder to readers, personas are fictitious characters who provide a realistic representation of a typical patient or nurse.

Figure 14-2. Detailed Patient Persona That We Culled From Empathy Mapping Efforts

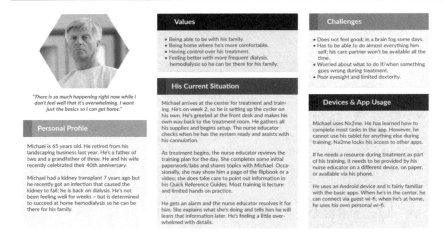

During the workshop, we reviewed the personas with the group. In our discussion we determined a need to further refine the personas because of the varying experience levels of patients and nurses in relationship to home hemodialysis. With the help of the patients and nurses in the room, we created three unique nurse personas and three patient personas to accommodate various beliefs and experiences with home hemodialysis. We encapsulated their personalities in simple-to-understand quotes. Figure 14-3 shows the patient version of these simplified personas.

Figure 14-3. Three Patient Personas

Movin' on Michael	**Incident Ian**	**Self-Care Sally**
"There is so much happening with my transition to HHD; it's overwhelming. I just want the basics so I can go home."	"I feel awful and crashed into dialysis. I don't understand how this is supposed to be my new normal?!?! It's hard to concentrate on this training with all of the other changes."	"I've got this down. After all, I've had experience with dialysis for years. I'm glad to be starting HHD; it will give me more control over my life."

Each persona has a simple-to-understand quote that illustrates their perspective on hemodialysis training. We also created three nurse personas that mirrored this style.

Table 14-3 lists factors discussed during the persona building that influenced the design.

Table 14-3. Patient and Nurse Educator Design Factors

Patient Factors	Nurse Educator Factors
Patients are typically older and usually very ill as they start home hemodialysis training; training materials need to be easy-to-read and simple to start and stop.	Nurses are busy completing multiple tasks even while training; the training materials need to be consolidated in one place to make them easier to manage.
The whole experience with dialysis is overwhelming because it completely changes their life; the training needs to acknowledge their new reality.	Experience and comfort with home hemodialysis and training varies from a new hire to someone nearing retirement; materials must adapt.
They typically rely on a phone if they use electronic devices; the training solution must be mobile-friendly.	Nurses most often use desktop computers, laptops, or tablets while working; the ideal app for them needs to work on these devices.

Verifying the Problem to Solve

We did not create formal problem statements as outlined in chapter 3. Instead we crafted simple statements from the point of view of the users: nurses and patients (Table 14-4). We asked, what problem are they having as opposed to what problem NxStage wants to solve from a business perspective?

Audience discussion during the workshop combined with prework analysis enabled us to verify the problem statements we wanted to focus on. Both statements assumed that key metrics involve keeping a higher percentage of patients on the therapy long-term and improving training efficiency, which lowers cost of training and increases capacity for training people.

Table 14-4. Problem and Goal Statements for Patients and Nurses

Problem Statements	Goal Statements
Patients: Training is inconsistent and overwhelming with disparate tools. I am struggling to be self-sufficient, which makes me feel less safe in my therapy.	NxLevel builds my confidence and competence. It gives me consistent, consolidated, and simple-to-understand support during training and when I'm home.
Nurses: I have no clear, easy-to-use and easy-to-access road map for how to train a patient from beginning to end.	NxLevel guides me in training a patient from beginning to end. It is easy to use and customizable, which helps me train patients comfortably, consistently, and efficiently.

Experience Mapping

After personas were crafted and problem and goal statements agreed upon, we began experience mapping. We divided participants into a patient group and a nurse group. Each group outlined its typical experience across three phases: pre-training, in-center training, and post-training.

The patient group broke down its experience in each phase into several steps. For each step, group members identified key activities the patient completes, along with potential miserable moments—and how to make those moments magical. During the pre-training phase for example, the group identified a gap in communication between patients and the nurse trainer while the patient decides if home hemodialysis is a good fit. This gap can leave patients feeling alone and fearful of the training experience until the next step. The training app became an obvious way to fill that gap and change the miserable moment to something more magical. The app could serve as an information source and offer a means of connecting with others going through training.

The nurse group followed the same process as the patient group. An example of miserable for this group was the difficulty in providing good continuity of care. Sometimes multiple nurses are involved in a patient's training. Nurse trainers find it challenging to pick up a patient's training program where another nurse left off. It's also difficult to fill in another nurse about where the patient is struggling, and how the patient is feeling about training. We were able to identify an opportunity to turn this miserable moment into a magical moment by designing the app to support easy customization of the training plan by patient and to make this training plan accessible to all nurses who interact with the patient as part of training.

Environmental and Technical Constraints

We had spirited conversation surrounding some tech specs. Technical constraints fall within the constraints circle of the Venn diagram that illustrates human-centered design (see chapter 2). We had strong discussions of what constraints of the environment or individuals influenced the specifications of the experience we designed. One huge issue was phones versus tablets. From the business's perspective, it was appealing to optimize the app for iPads and desktops. But during the design workshop, patients shared that they don't have iPads and likely wouldn't buy them just to use the app. At the same time, the group questioned whether a phone screen would be big enough to provide a great user experience. Patients' universal use of phones decided the issue, but our team had to pay careful attention to how we would scale complex training to fit on a phone screen (even plus-size phone screens!). Readability of content and easy navigation buttons would be top testing issues.

Going with a native or web app was another big decision point. Native apps are appealing because most people are familiar with how to download apps from the app store, and content is available offline. However, the burden of updating the app is on the user, and most users are notoriously bad about updating apps unless they experience problems with the app. Since medical science is constantly evolving, it's important that app updates get pushed to users. After asking design workshop attendees "How many of you have multiple app updates waiting on your phones right now?" and learning that a majority did, we decided to move forward with a responsive web app.

Other constraints we had to find solutions for included:

- the need to reuse the existing NxSteps content from 2010 as the essential topics of the training would remain unchanged
- patients not having email addresses to use in verifying accounts, resetting passwords, or creating accounts
- the need for the app to work across all types of phone devices.

Here are two constraints that we ended up either dismissing based on user feedback or working around:

- The need for a single app; we compromised on a web app that branched to accommodate the two audiences.
- The need for the app to be accessible via iPad or desktop. We ended up designing the patient app for the phone and the nurse app for the iPad and desktop.

Table 14-5 lists a few of the unique user stories by audience. The formula for creating these was: As a *[user type]*, I want to *[function]* so that *[benefit]*.

Table 14-5. Unique User Stories for Patients and Nurses

Patient Features	Nurse Features
As a patient, I want to . . . • See other patients explain what to expect with home hemodialysis so that my own concerns and anxieties are lessened. • Complete a self-assessment on readiness for home hemodialysis so that I can easily identify any areas of weakness. • Divide tasks between myself and my care partner so that I can focus on a smaller set of responsibilities. • Watch videos on topics like handwashing, cycler safety, self-cannulation, using the cycler and PureFlow, and responding to alarms so that I can see examples of good practices.	As a nurse, I want to . . . • Customize training plans for unique patients so that patients can focus on topics most relevant to them. • Access training materials including activity instructions, supply lists, and links to needed tools like reference guides, videos, and handouts so that I can efficiently provide relevant material to patients. • Track patient and care partner usage so that I have an automatically collected metric to help inform discussions. • Send NxStage questions and provide feedback on app content so that the app can continually improve based on user needs.

With a clear picture of our audience, goals, desired experience, and general features, we were ready to begin prototyping.

Creating the Learning Journeys and Initial Prototypes

After the workshop, we used all the contents from it (personas, experience maps, user stories, constraints) to generate an ideal learning or use journey for each group. The images that follow showcase elements of the patient and nurse journeys as well as a few images from each app that correspond to the journey. Beneath each image, we've summarized some highlights of that phase of the journey.

Figure 14-4. Pre-Training Portion of a Patient Journey

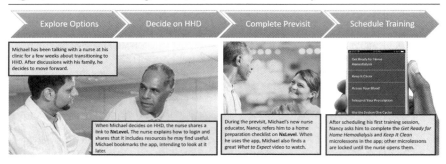

Pre-training journey highlights include the following:

- The app helps motivate and connect patients to their nurses and others in the broad home hemodialysis community. They learn what to expect.
- The app enables them to complete some initial training online before attending their first in-center, nurse-led session.
- The inclusion of what to expect came directly from what we heard from patients as they completed the experience map during the design workshop.

Figure 14-5. During-Training Portion of the Patient Journey

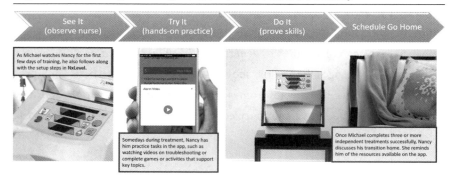

Highlights of the during-training journey included the following:

- All the content patients need to complete hands-on practice for setting up and completing treatment is housed in the app.

- The app includes videos, simple learning games, and reinforcement activities that patients can complete during their treatment sessions. This aspect of the journey reflected what we had learned about patients: Patients must be able to use the app with one hand while on treatment. This need for single-hand use influenced our screen layouts.

Figure 14-6. Patient App Map

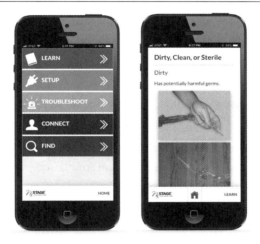

Early images of the patient app map to the experience we outlined in the patient learning journey.

In the nurses' journey, the app follows the same phased approach but includes considerably different features.

Figure 14-7. The Nurse's Pre-Training Journey With a Patient

Highlights of the pre-training journey for the nurse include:

- Functionality within the app that supports the administrative tasks the nurse must complete, including a streamlined patient setup that would give the nurse a positive impression of the app from their first use of it.
- Functionality within the app that enables the nurse to create a customized training plan for the patient based on what the nurse learns about the patient during the pre-training interview. This functionality—a "magical" moment for nurses—supported what we heard during the design workshop.

Figure 14-8. The Nurse's Journey During Training With a Patient

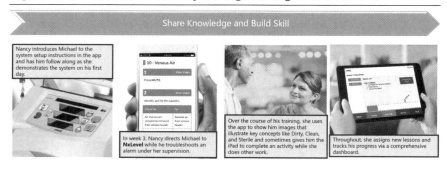

A highlight of this stage of the journey: Nurses needed a way to present content to patients as well a way to track progress during hands-on training with patients. From a miserable moment identified in the experience mapping, we knew nurses previously juggled multiple training tools; the app consolidated all materials into a single source. Tracking progress across the multi-week training experience was a manual job so we designed the app to include robust reporting.

Figure 14-9. Images of the Nurse's App, Designed for iPad

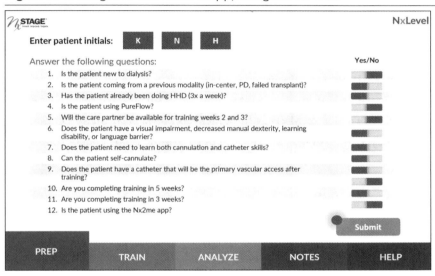

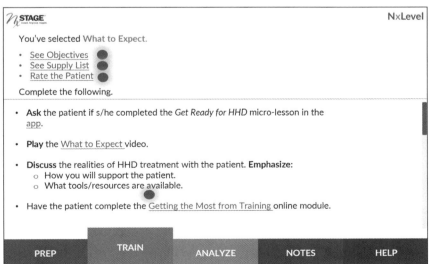

The top image shows the patient customization feature; the bottom image shows what a training plan looks like for the start of the training day.

In addition to mapping out the learning journeys, we also built simple prototypes that users could test. Their feedback on initial prototypes informed our subsequent development.

Moving Into Development: User Testing and MVP

We wanted users involved every step of the way. We learned a lesson from the bulky binders we made in 2010. We had numerous content review sessions as we developed materials in 2010, but we did not test those materials in actual dialysis centers or have nurse educators use them and give feedback until we got to pilot stage. With this redo, we wanted feedback as we went along.

We organized development into three-week sprints. We released a minimum viable product, or MVP, at the conclusion of each sprint and conducted user testing with NxStage patients and nurse trainers. The goal of the testing was to assess usability, value, and appeal. Figure 14-10 shows the simple testing matrix we used each time. If a tester rated something medium or low, we asked them what would make the rating adjust to high.

Figure 14-10. User Testing Matrix

	Rate each item High, Medium, Low. Explain your ratings.		
Rating Items	**Aesthetic Appeal**	**Clarity ("I get how to do stuff")**	**Overall Usefulness or Value of App**
Tester 1	High	High	High
Tester 2	High	High	High
Tester 3	Medium—want more visual interest, like background graphicsd	High	High
Tester 4	High	High	High

Testing prompted many changes as we progressed, all for the better. One example occurred as we tested the first prototype (Figure 14-11). The top image shows the slider format we used for the initial survey; we used gray and blue colors for the slider. During usability testing, nurses said that it wasn't clear to them which position on the slider was Yes and which was No. We adjusted the next release of the app to what is shown in the bottom image.

Figure 14-11. Improving User Experience

Top image: The slider bars weren't intuitive to nurses. They couldn't tell which position indicated Yes answers and which indicated a No answer. *Bottom image:* We eliminated slider bars entirely and went with the words Yes/No. We also made Yes button turn green when selected so nurses got a visual and text-based cue.

Our focus throughout development was optimizing the user experience. Small changes like the one we just described can have a huge impact on an app's adoption.

Key development and testing strategies we used included:

- Conducting testing separately for each user group—one call for patients and one for nurses.
- Zeroing in on areas during testing where we needed to do A/B testing or send mockups. A/B testing means we tested two different versions to see which version had more positive results.
- Focusing on gathering feedback from actual target users. This project included many stakeholders who were not target users. While they had a stake in the project, they couldn't relate directly to how the app would impact their daily lives. These individuals attended regular higher-level steering committee meetings instead of usability tests so that they could stay up to date without getting into the weeds. If we did get usability feedback from a stakeholder, we checked in with our target users.
- Keeping the end in mind: We wanted an app that was intuitive and easy for nurses and patients so that they are motivated to keep using it.

The supporting structure for these strategies was stakeholders who bought into the process and agreed to put users in the driver's seat. NxStage did an excellent job of this, and it paid dividends. By our last usability testing call, both testing groups were so excited for this to be live because they felt they had created something extremely intuitive and valuable. Consult chapter 10 on getting buy-in from stakeholders on a new process, and use the case study in this chapter or chapter 13 (or use one of your own) to win them over.

Acknowledgments

Sharon

This is my third book; it was, by far, the hardest to write. A lot was going on in my life as I wrote it—including the very major transition from owning a business to selling a business to becoming part of the business that bought my company.

My husband Kirk deserves the first and most massive thank you. He endured a lot of less-than best-self me as I endeavored to get these chapters written on nights and weekends . . . and then rewrote because the original chapters weren't solid enough. Kirk—thank you for supporting me, for never raising your eyebrows at me when I whined about the late nights and weekends. Thank you for the hot meals that "magically" appeared while I worked and for the lack of commentary about the lost nights and weekends together.

Thank you to my co-author Laura. I talked her into co-authoring with me, and I suspect she may have had second or third thoughts once things got rolling. It was a giant leap for her. She handled the challenge with grace and zeal. She was also willing to be my thought partner before this book even took shape. She eagerly accepted the challenge when I told her I wanted to integrate design thinking techniques into how we executed our work.

A huge thank you to Leigh Mortier from NxStage and to Cynthia Hinman from CAISO for helping us with the case studies. It can be a challenge going through the hoops of securing legal permissions. Both of you were so gracious in your willingness to tackle those hoops and allow us to share your stories. It's greatly appreciated. It benefits us as authors, but it benefits the readers far more as examples are priceless.

Thank you to my new colleagues and friends at TiER1 Performance for giving me the space I needed to finish this book. Without your willingness to simply let me take several days' time to focus 100 percent on the book, I'm not sure it would have reached completion. A special thank you to Nick

Paneda and Dustin Shell, who gave me permission to incorporate the "How might we?" example as well as the "5-Minute Think" that I saw them use as part of a workshop they delivered. I get new ideas on techniques all the time from watching others; I'm not inventing them. I'm discovering examples from amazing industry colleagues like Dustin and Nick.

Thank you, Justin Brusino, for recommending me as the author for this topic. I appreciate the vote of confidence. Thank you, Eliza Blanchard, for stepping in to shepherd this book midstream and bring it to publication. It's a long journey; I appreciate you hanging in there for it.

Finally, thank you, thank you Jack Harlow. You helped shape this book with your thoughtful editing and gentle nudges. You worked hard with us to ensure this book was the best book it could be.

Laura

I am so thankful to have had the opportunity to collaborate on this book and for all the people who made that a possibility:

I am ever grateful to my husband Luke, who is the best thing that ever happened to me. Unsurprisingly, twin five-year-olds are not conducive to book-writing, and you never hesitated to give me the time and space I needed (which was a lot). Thank you for always, always, always being in my corner.

Sharon, thank you for inviting me on this journey with you. The passion and experience you bring to the plate every day fuels my fire! I always appreciate the way you challenge me to think differently, broaden my perspective, and expand my skill set; this book is a perfect example of that.

Special thanks to Cindy Hinman at CAISO for your trust and support with this book and throughout the big, beautiful curricula we've built together. Thank you for sharing your hands-on approach to project management and for your constant partnership at each step of the way.

To Jack Harlow, our talented editor. Thank you for your clear vision of the destination and your patience on our way there.

Finally, to the incredible team at Bottom-Line Performance: Thank you for your brilliance, your willingness to experiment and learn together, your passion, and constant push to take things to the next level. You are inspiring.

APPENDIXES

Appendix 1

Learning Journey Worksheet

This journey map works best when formatted horizontally. For the purposes of this book, we've adjusted it to fit the vertical page. Feel free to reproduce this as a horizontal image so you can create wider columns. You may also want to create it using sticky notes with flipchart pages for each column if you are doing this as part of a design meeting.

Phase	Prepare		Acquire Knowledge and Skill	Built Memory and Try Using on the Job		Maintain Over Time
Step	Notice	Commit	Learn and Practice	Repeat and Elaborate	Reflect and Explore	Sustain Usage
Desired Outcomes	Accept the need to learn.	Make time to learn.	Engage, find relevance.	Remain committed; gain confidence.	Go deeper; learn more; share early successes.	Consistently use new skill or knowledge; achieve business results.
Key Actions or Activities						
Thoughts and Feelings						
Magical Moments						
Miserable Moments						

Appendix 2

Blank Strategy Blueprint

This strategy blueprint works best when formatted horizontally. For the purposes of this book, we've adjusted it to fit the vertical page. A couple of the questions beneath categories are tweaked for a training and development context. When we use these maps, we create them on a wall and have design meeting participants use sticky notes to respond to prompts or to document comments we hear as we facilitate the meeting.

Revisit chapter 9 to see an example of a completed blueprint.

Challenges What problems are you trying to solve? What obstacles must you overcome?			
Aspirations What does success look like? What will people do, say, or perform differently?	**Focus Areas** What is the scope of the solution? What will you focus on for the most impact?	**Guiding Principles** How will you overcome the challenges? What specific mantras will guide teams as they develop the solution?	**Activities** What types of activities solve the problem? What capabilities achieve your aspirations?
		Outcomes What metrics will be used to gauge success? What types of measures will you use?	

Used with permission from Jim Kalbach.

Appendix 3

Sample Observation Guide

Directions: Spend five to 15 minutes introducing yourself to the observed employee. Get clarity on their role. During the observation, ask them to think out loud as they complete various tasks. Complete the first three sections—General, Environment, and Workflow.

General

Site: _____

Time: _____

Department: Production Engineering Marketing Sales

Manager: Yes No

Employee Name and Role: _____

Environment

Describe general work environment (location, noise level, busyness, etc.)

Describe technology tools used, including length of time engaged (e.g. "cell phone, 20 min call, 10 min text").

List collaborative partners (who the employees interacted with and how they worked together).

List any on-the-job support resources the employee accessed. How did they access it? What was the employee hoping to learn?

Workflow

Outline the key tasks you observed the employee complete in 15-minute increments. Make notes of any **tools** used, **people** they collaborated with, **key quotes** they said while performing the task, and any other unique observations about their **experiences**.

	Task	Additional Observations and Key Quotes
15		
30		
45		
60		

Appendix 4

Note: This sample guide is targeted to front desk hotel employees to learn what content should be included in a new onboarding program. It includes a combination of qualitative and quantitative questions. You can use this as a starting template when creating interview guides of your own.

Interviewee name and role: _____

Purpose: The purpose of this interview is to gather information to guide the design of sales training for hotel staff. We would like your input so that the training is successful and meets your needs.

Background Information

First, we want to ask you some information about your background and how things currently work in your hotel.

Question	Response
How long have you been in your role? Tell me a little bit about your background.	
What are the most important parts of your job? Why do you say that?	

Current Sales Process and Training

Next, we want to talk to you a bit about how the sales process works at your location and what you think the highest needs are for people in your role.

Question	Response
On a scale of 1-10, how would you rate your skill level at taking reservation calls? (10 being "I've heard it all," and 1 being "I hope the phone doesn't ring")	
How does shift or time of day affect your ability to handle reservation calls? Can you give me an example?	
What sales training have you taken? What did you think of it?	
Have you received any coaching or other kinds of support related to sales at this hotel?	
If yes, what kinds?	

Content Analysis

Now we'd like to hear from you about which topics you think are most important to include in the training and how you think the ideal sales call should proceed.

Think about the existing sales training. We will list the topics currently included in the training. For each topic, tell us **how important it is for a new employee to learn** on a scale of 1-10, with 10 being critical to learn, and 1 being not necessary to learn. After the rating: **What, if anything, would you add, subtract, or change to improve this list?**	Training Topic	Rating	Notes
	Important local client groups		
	Features and benefits of this property		
	The reservations program		

Now let's talk about reservation calls. We will list call attributes. For each attribute, tell us **how important it is to ask or say on a call** on a scale of 1-10, with 10 being critical to ask or say on a call, and 1 being not necessary to ask or say. After the rating: **What, if anything, would you add, subtract, or change to improve this list?**	Call Attribute	Rating	Notes
	Greeting		
	Use a friendly phone voice.		
	Qualification of needs		
	Determine the purpose of travel.		
	Ask for negotiated rate.		
	Ask number of people in the party.		
	Ask for special requests.		
	Ask if client is a loyalty member.		
	Presentation		
	Describe a feature of the property without prompting.		
	Describe a benefit statement when presenting the feature.		
	Select features specific to the individual client's needs or type of stay.		
	Discuss the loyalty program.		
	Describe a feature of the property without prompting.		
	Closing		
	Ask to book the reservation.		
	Repeat all information back to the guest.		
	Explain the cancellation policy.		
	Offer confirmation number.		
	Ask for client's email address.		
	End call with friendly conclusion.		

If you had to choose the three most important things a new employee should learn about sales, what would those be?	
What else is important for us to know as we design the sales training for hotel staff?	

Conclusion

Would it be OK if we reach out to you later in the project with further questions or ideas?

Thank you very much for helping us design an effective training experience!

Appendix 5

Blank Empathy Map

Feel free to photocopy this map or locate one online by searching for "empathy map templates." You can use this to mockup an empathy map on a whiteboard or flipchart paper as well.

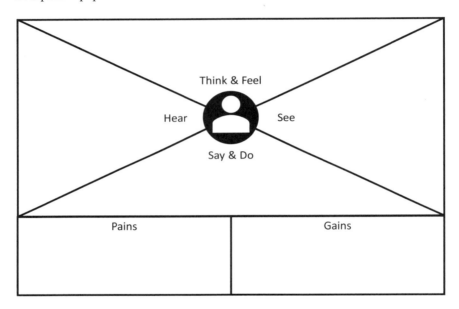

Appendix 6

Experience Map Template

This template can be expanded to include as many columns as you need. We often use sticky notes for column and row headings and do this exercise along a wall.

Major Tasks	Key Phases, Tasks, or Steps		
	Task 1	Task 2	Task 3
Actions Taken			
Timing/Frequency			
Thoughts and Feelings While Doing			
Challenges, Distractions, or Common Mistakes			
What Sets Apart a Star Performer			
Magical or Miserable Moments			

Appendix 7

Sample DIF Worksheet

Difficulty, Importance, Frequency (DIF) analyses can be hugely helpful in identifying what parts of a job should be addressed via training and which should be addressed via some sort of just-in-time resource. To complete a DIF worksheet, you ask learners to rate the difficulty, importance, and frequency of a task on a scale of low, medium, and high.

Here are some general guidelines for interpreting your results; you can decide if and when to deviate from these based on your analysis results:

- Tasks that are of high importance and difficulty but that learners perform with low frequency (highlighted in the table below) should be prioritized for formal training and just-in-time support so that when the need for the task arises, the performer is well prepared. Example: CPR for lifeguards: It's done infrequently, but it takes practice to do correctly and has life-or-death consequences if done incorrectly. You will also see poster displays and other job aids in settings where CPR is likely to be performed as a reminder of key steps. Fire drills are performed annually to practice in exiting the building. In addition, you will see "In the event of an emergency" posters displayed by elevators and stairways as reminders of the correct evacuation procedure to follow.

- Tasks performed with high frequency but low difficulty or importance might be things people can work through as they execute their jobs. Consider whether on-the-job learning is sufficient for these to allow training efforts to focus on more critical skills. Example: Communicating via collaboration software such as Microsoft Teams. Assuming the program is used multiple times a day, training resources are likely not necessary to learn basic functionalities.

- You can create a DIF worksheet for almost any type of skill, including soft skills, problem-solving skills, selling skills, and so on. It's a great way to help everyone recognize what level of support and training is optimal. The sample here is an excerpt for an analysis of what sales reps need to do in Salesforce Lightning.

Category	Task	Difficulty	Importance	Frequency
Set up	Import all leads and opportunities	H	H	L
Set up	Import all notes	M	H	L
Set up	Import all tasks	M	H	L
Reporting	Access and understand sales reports	L	H	H
Reporting	Generate and access general reports	L	M	M
Dashboards	Set up a company dashboard	H	H	L
Dashboards	Set up a personal dashboard	M	M	L
Leads	Create new leads	L	H	H
Leads	Create new lead views	L	H	H

Appendix 8

Identifying and Verifying Constraints

Directions: Think about a recent or current project you have. Use the worksheet below to consider the constraints you have identified in each of the categories. Then see if you are assuming these are constraints or if you have verified them. If you haven't verified them, see if you can identify who might help you do so.

Constraint	Specifics of constraint	Verified?	Who Can Verify?
Budget		__Yes __ No	
Time		__Yes __ No	
Technology		__Yes __ No	
People		__Yes __ No	
Environment		__Yes __ No	

Appendix 9

Sample Pilot Evaluation Tool

We used Will Thalheimer's book, Performance-Focused Smile Sheets, *to help us craft this pilot evaluation tool for a women's leadership program called Women's Leadership Forum (WLF). We combined written evaluation with an oral debrief focused on elements that participants found most valuable and what they recommended we start, stop, and continue doing with future cohorts based on their own experiences. Data gathered from this pilot helped inform subsequent versions of the program.*

Directions: Please circle your response below. If you want to refresh yourself on any program components, the final two pages of this handout include a summary. (Program summary omitted from this example tool.)

Overall Experience

1. Looking back at WLF, how well do you feel you understand the concepts taught? CHOOSE ONE.

   a) I am still at least SOMEWHAT CONFUSED about the concepts.

   b) I am now SOMEWHAT FAMILIAR WITH the concepts.

   c) I have a SOLID UNDERSTANDING of the concepts.

   d) I AM FULLY READY TO USE the concepts in my work.

   e) I have an EXPERT-LEVEL ABILITY to use the concepts.

Please explain your answer. We welcome feedback on what you feel you understand best and least:

2. HOW ABLE ARE YOU to put what you learned as part of the program into practice in your work? CHOOSE ONE OPTION that best describes your current readiness.

   a) My CURRENT ROLE DOES NOT ENABLE me to use what I learned.

   b) I AM STILL UNCLEAR about what to do, or why to do it.

   c) I NEED MORE GUIDANCE before I know how to use what I learned.

   d) I NEED MORE EXPERIENCE to be good at using what I learned.

   e) I CAN BE SUCCESSFUL NOW in using what I learned (even without more guidance or experience).

   f) I CAN PERFORM NOW AT AN EXPERT LEVEL in using what I learned.

3. How have you or will you apply what you learned in WLF to your work or your role as a leader?

4. Based on your experience, was attending WLF a good use of your time: yes or no? If no, why not?

5. Aside from the learning opportunities, how else did WLF provide value to you?

6. What could have been done better to make this a more effective learning experience?

Program Specifics

7. Circle ALL the items that you felt added value to the program experience. Place a star beside the item of GREATEST value to you.

a) Workshop sessions with outside facilitator

b) Mentoring Circle meetings

c) One-on-one connections

d) *No Ceiling, No Walls* book

e) *Emotional Intelligence 2.0* book and self-assessment

f) *Strength Finders* book and self-assessment

g) Text messaging tool that sent reminders to you

Appendix 10

Implementation Plan Template

Use this simple tool to create a summary of your rollout plan for your initiative.

Key stakeholders and their stake in successful implementation			
Stakeholder #1 name, project role, description of their stake in success of implementation. (Note: Learners are a stakeholder. List them here.)			
Stakeholder #2 name	Stakeholder #3 name	Stakeholder #4 name	

Targeted outcomes	Who, how, and when will we measure?		
Outcome 1	Include individual's name, role, method of measurement, and timepoint for measuring.		
Outcome 2 (add rows as needed)			

Risks to implementation success	Risk Level			How will we mitigate high or medium risks?
Risk 1	High	Med	Low	Description of mitigating strategy
Risk 2	High	Med	Low	
Risk 3 (add rows as needed)	High	Med	Low	

Milestones and key tasks*	Target date	Who is accountable	Who is involved
Milestone 1 (for example, a pilot event)			
Task 1			
Task 2 (Add rows as needed)			
Milestone 2			
Task 1			
Task 2 (Add rows as needed)			
Repeat milestones and task lists as needed.			

Tips for Documenting Milestones and Tasks

- Be granular enough that your milestones and key tasks help everyone in your organization grasp what's involved in implementation. Critical activities that are part of each stage of the learning journey belong in this section of the plan. For almost all the learner activities within a learning journey, there will be associated actions on the organizational side. If learners are the target of a pre-event marketing campaign, for example, the organization must distribute the messages. If there are multiple messages spread out over a period of days or weeks, then put the distribution of each message on its own task line so the effort doesn't get minimized.

- Include monitoring checkpoints and measurement checkpoints. This is the most frequently overlooked aspect of implementation: monitoring and measuring progress and acting on deviations from target goals.

- If you plan to do a pilot or roll an initiative out in waves, specify each wave as a milestone. For example, perhaps you are rolling out a program nationwide. You plan to start in a single city for the pilot of your initiative and then roll out by regions of the country. Include a milestone for the pilot, region 1, region 2, and so on. You will likely have monitoring and measurement milestones interspersed between these waves so you can assess and you go and recalibrate, if needed.

- Be very careful about assigning accountability to a group or a function; it's always better to assign it to a specific person or role. Others may be involved, but only one role or individual should have ultimate accountability for a task or milestone.

Appendix 11

The Learning-Transfer Evaluation Model

Abbreviated as LTEM (Pronounced "L-tem")

Tier 8	Effects of Transfer	Effects of Transfer: Including outcomes affecting (a) learners, (b) coworkers/ family/friends, (c) organization, (d) community, (e) society, and (f) the environs. *CERTIFYING EFFECTS OF TRANSFER REQUIRES: Certification of transfer plus a rigorous method of assessing transfer's causal impact—including positive and negative effects.*
7	Transfer	When learner uses what was learned to perform work tasks successfully—as clearly demonstrated through objective measures. Assisted Transfer—when performance is substantially prompted/supported. *ADEQUATE TO CERTIFY ASSISTED TRANSFER.* Full Transfer—when learner demonstrates full agency in applying the learning. *ADEQUATE TO CERTIFY FULL TRANSFER.*
6	Task Competence	Learner performs relevant realistic actions and decision making. Task Competence—during or right after learning event. *Not a fully adequate metric because learners may forget their task competencies.* Remembered Task Competence—after several days or more. *ADEQUATE TO CERTIFY TASK COMPETENCE.* *NOTE: "Tasks" comprise both decision making and action taking. For example, a person learning to write poetry could decide to use metaphor, could act to use it, or could do both.*
5	Decision Making Competence	Learner makes decisions given relevant realistic scenarios. Decision Making Competence—during or right after learning event. *Not a fully adequate metric because learners may forget decision making competencies.* Remembered Decision Making Competence—after several days or more. *ADEQUATE TO CERTIFY DECISION MAKING COMPETENCE.*

4	Knowledge	Learner answers questions about facts/terminology. Knowledge Recitation—during or right after learning event. *Usually inadequate because knowing terminology does not fully enable performance.* Knowledge Retention—after several days or more. *Usually inadequate because remembering terminology does not fully enable performance.*
3	Learner Perceptions	A. Learner is queried in a way that reveals insights related to learning effectiveness. Examples: Measures that target Learner Comprehension, Realistic Practice, Learner Motivation to Apply, After-Learning Support, etc. *Such measures can hint at outcomes but should be augmented with objective outcome measures.*
		B. Learner is queried in a way that does NOT reveal insights on learning effectiveness. Examples: Measures that target Learner Satisfaction, Course Reputation, etc. *A metric inadequate to validate learning success—because such perceptions are not always related to learning results.*
2	Activity	Learner engages in activities related to learning. Measures of Attention *A metric inadequate to validate learning success—because learners may pay attention but not learn.* Measures of Interest *A metric inadequate to validate learning success—because learners may show interest but not learn.* Measures of Participation *A metric inadequate to validate learning success—because learners may participate but not learn.*
1	Attendance	Learner signs up, starts, attends, or completes a learning experience. *A metric inadequate to validate learning success—because learners may attend but not learn.*

Appendix 12

Evaluation Exercise

Directions: Think about a learning experience in which you participated. Reflect on the following questions, and document your answers:

- What activities occurred at each step of the learning journey, starting with learn?
- Which metrics might have been effective for evaluating the successful completion of the learning journey? (It is not necessary to have one for every step; decide which activities would yield the most meaningful data.)
- Refer to the LTEM model in appendix 11. Which tier does each metric correlate with?

	Learn	Repeat and Elaborate	Reflect and Explore	Sustain
Learning Activities				
Metrics				
LTEM Tier #				

Appendix 13

Sample Cost Analysis Worksheet

We've included two samples to show how you might illustrate the costs associated with development and rolling out a training initiative. Build your own worksheet by using Excel or Google Sheets.

Both examples show learners' time to participate in training is the biggest impact on the organization. The time needed from a few learners upfront to provide perspective is very small; the cumulative time the entire population of learners will spend going through the learning experience is high. Use this data to help you illustrate how a small investment upfront helps protect the much larger investment the company makes in having a huge segment of people go through training. Making the invisible visible often helps you secure funding and gain agreement on metrics you will use to measure success.

Note: These simple worksheets do not capture the total financial impact of an initiative. Other costs include lost opportunity and inefficiency if training doesn't help someone perform better or maintain performance. These worksheets also don't show the cost of time not spent doing the employee's normal duties. For example, if a sales rep is in training, they are not selling to customers. If the training time doesn't yield skill gains, then it's a double loss for the company.

Example 1: Large-Scale Initiative

Section 1: Internal People Costs					
Project role	Salary used	Estimated hours	Cost per hour	Total cost	Assumptions affecting cost estimate
Internal L&D consultant	$90,000	100	$54	$5,400	Project manager internally: liaison with external consultant's team
VP of Sales	$200,000	16	$42	$1,920	Sponsor; high-level involvement only
Content SME/ reviewer #1	$70,000	40	$120	$1,680	Key reviewer and content provider
Content SME/ reviewer #2	$100,000	24	$60	$1,440	Key reviewer and content provider
Brand reviewer	$90,000	16	$54	$864	Reviews to ensure consistency with brand guidelines and messaging
Provider of learner perspective during design	$150,000	12	$120	$1,440	Assumes three sales reps support design with interviews and participation in a design meeting.
Learners	$150,000	4000	$120	$480,000	Time is spread across six months; target is 250 sales reps.
Subtotal hours and cost		4208		$492,74	

Section 2: External Costs		
Description	**Fees**	**Assumptions affecting cost estimate**
Consultant fees	$ 200,000	Consultant designs and develops e-learning + live event and post-event materials.
Media production	$50,000	Up to 15 minutes of video
Printing/reproduction	$5,000	Participant guides and workshop materials for 250 ppl
Subtotal	$255,000	
Ballpark company investment	$747,744.00	

Tips for creating section 1 of this worksheet:

- Focus on the primary roles involved and consider time required to attend meetings, review drafts, coordinate and work with others, and generate project summaries and updates. If your role is the project manager, make sure you add sufficient time for working directly with any external team members, such as a consulting firm.
- To ensure you are thinking of everything, use the Assumptions affecting cost estimate column to explain the factors you considered when determining hours of effort involved, the salary choice, or the role included.
- You can either use the table we provide within this appendix as your means of estimating the actual hourly cost by role or you can talk to someone within your HR function. They should have general hourly costs for a specific role (not a person, but a role).

Example 2: Small-Scale Internal Initiative

Internal People Costs					
Project role	Salary used	Estimated hours	Cost per hour	Total cost	Assumptions affecting cost estimate
Internal L&D consultant; developer of solution	$90,000	200	$54	$10,800	One-stop shop for creating a solution—does it all. Solution = 30-minute e-learning course plus some job aids.
VP of business unit	$200,000	8	$120	$960	Sponsor; high-level involvement only
Content SME and reviewer	$70,000	40	$42	$ 1,680	Key reviewer and content provider
Provider of learner perspective during design	$70,000	10	$42	$420	Assumes up to five employees affected by safety chance are included in design discussions and solution testing
Learners	$70,000	250	$42	$10,500	All 500 employees in company get training as it is related to safety related. Used $70 thousand to represent average across all salaries in company
Total investment		502		$24,360	

"Load" Added for Benefits and Taxes

Annual Salary	Hourly rate	25% "load"	Total hourly cost	Formula explanation
$ 50,000	24	6	$30	To get an
$ 70,000	34	8	$42	hourly rate
$ 90,000	43	11	$54	divide annual
$100,000	48	12	$60	salary by 2080 hours.
$125,000	60	15	$75	2080 = 52
$150,000	72	18	$90	weeks x 40
$200,000	96	24	$120	hours/week.

Appendix 14

How to Apply Design Thinking Midstream

Think of one project that is already in progress or even already launched. Use the strategies defined in chapter 12 and fill in the template below to create a step-by-step action plan for applying design thinking to that project.

	Who is included in this step?	Target start date	Target end date	Intended outcome
Project name: **Project status:** (circle one) • Design is drafted • Development has begun • Pilot-ready • Post-launch				
Step 1:				
Step 2:				
Step 3:				
Step 4:				

References and Resources

ABC News. 2011. "Embrace Infant Warmer Could Save Lives." September 12. youtube.com/watch?v=-PyY94ssSww.

Association for Talent Development (ATD). 2016. *Evaluating Learning: Getting to Measurements That Matter*. Alexandria, VA: ATD Press.

Boller, S., and S. Boller. 2019. *2019 Learning Trends Report*. New Palestine, IN: Bottom-Line Performance.

Brinkerhoff, R. 2003. *The Success Case Method: Find Out Quickly What's Working and What's Not*. San Francisco: Berrett-Koehler Publishers.

Dietz, D. 2012. "Transforming Healthcare for Children and Their Families." Delivered at TEDx, San Jose, CA. youtube.com/watch?v=jajduxPD6H4.

Dikes, B. 2016. "Why Do We Frequently Question Data but Not Assumptions?" Forbes, June 16.

Kalbach, J. 2014. "UX Strategy Blueprint." Experiencing Information (blog), August 12. experiencinginformation.com/2014/08/12/ux-strategy-blueprint.

Kalbach, J. 2016. *Mapping Experiences: A Complete Guide to Creating Value Through Journeys, Blueprints, and Diagrams*. Sebastopol, CA: O'Reilly Media.

Karpicke, J., and H.L. Roedinger III. 2008. "The Critical Importance of Retrieval for Learning." Science 319:5865.

Kirkpatrick, J.D., and W.K. Kirkpatrick. 2016. *Kirkpatrick's Four Levels of Training Evaluation*. Alexandria, VA: ATD Press.

McGrath, R.G. 2016. "The Destructive Power of Assumptions." Fortune, July 13.

Medina, J. 2014. *Brain Rules*. Seattle, WA: Pear Press.

Murayama, K. 2018. "The Science of Motivation." *Psychological Science Agenda*, June.

Phillips, P.P., and J.J. Phillips. 2019. *ROI Basics*, 2nd ed. Alexandria, VA: ATD Press.

ROI Institute. n.d. "The ROI Methodology Process Model." ROI Institute Free Tools. roiinstitute.net/download/the-roi-methodology-a-brief-overview.

Stanford University. 2008. "Embrace." Extreme Designs for Extreme Affordability, June 20. extreme.stanford.edu/projects/embrace.

Thalheimer, W. 2016. *Performance-Based Smile Sheets*. Boston: Work-Learning Press.

Thalheimer, W. 2018. "The Learning-Transfer Evaluation Model: Sending Messages to Enable Learning Effectiveness." Work-Learning Research, October 5. worklearning.com/ltem.

UCLA Bjork Learning and Forgetting Lab. n.d. "Applying Cognitive Psychology to Enhance Educational Practice." Bjork Lab Research. bjorklab.psych.ucla.edu/research.

Helpful Resources

Books

Brown, T. 2009. *Change By Design*. New York: Harper Collins.

Garrette, B., C. Phelps, and O. Sibony. 2018. *Cracked It! How to Solve Big Problems and Sell Solutions Like Top Strategy Consultants*. London: Palgrave Macmillan.

Kalbach, J. 2016. *Mapping Experiences: A Complete Guide to Creating Value Through Journeys, Blueprints, and Diagrams*. Sebastopol, CA: O'Reilly Media.

Kirkpatrick, J.D., and W.K. Kirkpatrick. 2016. *Kirkpatrick's Four Levels of Training Evaluation*. Alexandria, VA: ATD Press.

Online Resources

Interaction Design Foundation: interaction-design.org

Learning Battle Cards: learningbattlecards.com

Luma Institute: interaction-design.org

The IDEO.org design kit website: designkit.org

The Stanford d.school Design Thinking Bootleg: dschool.stanford.edu/resources/design-thinking-bootleg

Index

Page numbers followed by *f* or *t* refer to figures or tables, respectively.

About the Authors

Sharon Boller

Sharon Boller is a managing director at TiER1 Performance, where she focuses on helping clients figure out how to activate their business strategies through their people. She partners with her colleagues at TiER1 to bring together the disciplines of learning, change, communication, technology, and creativity to create blended solutions that enable people to do their best work.

Prior to joining TiER1 Performance, Sharon was the CEO and president of Bottom-Line Performance (BLP), a learning solutions firm she founded in 1995. She and her partner/co-owner Kirk Boller grew BLP from a single-woman sole proprietorship to a $4 million-plus company with a highly skilled team of diverse capabilities. Under the direction of Sharon and Kirk, BLP produced communication, education, and training solutions for life science companies, manufacturing, energy companies, and more.

Sharon is a frequent speaker at industry conferences on topics such as performance-focused learning design, UX, technology and trends, learning game design, and design thinking. She is the author of two other books published by ATD Press: *Teamwork Training* was published in 1995, and *Play to Learn: Everything You Need to Know About Designing Effective Learning Games* was published in 2017 with co-author Karl Kapp. Her company is the recipient of more than 30 awards from organizations such as Brandon Hall, Horizon Interactive Awards, and Life Science Trainers and Educators Network.

Her industry interests are wide-ranging and include storytelling, emerging technologies, business strategy, leadership, learning, and experience design.

Laura Fletcher

Laura Fletcher is a seasoned learning consultant with 15 years' experience in learning and development. She served the clients of Bottom-Line Performance for over seven years, where she designed and developed award-winning solutions ranging from instructor-led workshops to mobile apps. It was during her tenure as manager of Instructional Design at Bottom-Line Performance that her ID team became something of a design-thinking "incubation lab," experimenting with design thinking techniques and integrating them into the design process.

After leaving Bottom-Line Performance, she joined Salesforce, where she consults with leaders and teams to cultivate advancement- and leadership-readiness. She continues to rely on design thinking to ensure programming meets the needs of thousands of diverse, global employees while also delivering value to the business.

She has a master's degree in Human Resource Development from the University of Illinois and lives in Indianapolis with her husband and two children.